D0871245

OREMUS

OREMUS

Collects, Devotions, Litanies
From Ancient and Modern
Sources

EDITED BY

PAUL ZELLER STRODACH

AUGSBURG PUBLISHING HOUSE
MINNEAPOLIS   7298   MINNESOTA

OREMUS

Library of Congress Catalog Card No. 66-13049

This volume, originally published in 1925 by the
United Lutheran Publication House, is reprinted by
permission of Fortress Press, Philadelphia.

FOREWORD

This new edition of a long-loved book of prayers is issued in the hope that another generation of Christian people, clergy and lay alike, will find in it the same spiritual treasures which an earlier generation found.

It is still true that
"Prayer is the soul's sincere desire,
Unuttered or expressed."
And it is equally true that the God-ward aspirations which one Christian finds difficulty in expressing have found expression in the words of another. That is what gives validity to prayer books. They do not replace the spontaneous outpourings of the individual in his "free prayers." They supplement them.

Paul Zeller Strodach was a compiler and editor rather than an author. The series of sermon books which he compiled and edited, for example, were widely used. *Oremus*, too, is a compilation. Into it went a stupendous amount of research in the devotional literature of classical Christianity. But, more than that, he was a man who himself knew that literature as few have. If it is appropriate to speak of a given prayer as "having been tested," then we may say that the prayers in this book had been tested in the compiler's prayer life.

While a few sections of *Oremus* are particularly intended for the use of pastors, the great majority of the prayers are equally applicable to the prayer life of pew and pulpit. For that matter, the congregation may well make the pastor's prayers for himself their prayers for him.

In his Foreword to the first edition of *Oremus*, the late Dr. Henry Eyster Jacobs wrote, "In brief compass, there is here condensed the fruit of many years' study of the church's rich devotional literature and its practical use in the pastoral office and in the preparation of devotional Orders of Service. The editor, having caught the spirit of this literature, now humbly offers his own additions to what has long been the common property of the church. For wherever there is life there is growth; and the question may well be asked whether, as Christian people, we fully avail ourselves of the privilege of prayer, when besides the comprehensive petitions, whose value all acknowledge, special petitions for particular objects or with reference to peculiar circumstances be not also included."

O. G. MALMIN

CONTENTS

PREFACE 9

PREPARATORY COLLECTS 13

COLLECTS AND PRAYERS.................... 15

  Brief Prayers and Aspirations........... 15

COLLECTS (GENERAL AND PERSONAL)....... 21

  For the Church......................... 67
  For Family and Friends................. 78
  For the Sick........................... 83
  For Those for Whom I Should Pray..... 88
  General Prayers 96
  Morning Prayers 104
  Evening Prayers 112

IN PREPARATION FOR PARISH WORK........ 118

IN CONNECTION WITH DIVINE SERVICE..... 126

SHORT OFFICE BEFORE ENTERING THE
  SANCTUARY 134

IN THE SANCTUARY...................... 136

LITANIES 156

  Litany for Matins..................... 156
  Litany of the Most Holy Name of Jesus.. 158

Litany of the Passion 163
Litany of the Holy Sacrament 167
Litany of the Holy Ghost 171
Litany of Intercession 177
Litany for the Sick 185
Litany for the Dying 189
SOURCES 191

PREFACE

Dominus vobiscum—
Sursum corda—
Oremus—*Let us pray!*

As the years are laid away in the storehouse of the past and with them the memories of the throngs, ever growing, who have completed their journey under the banner of the cross, we who are still journeying find that what they have left us is not all "History," that what they were and what they have done are not all "Memories," but living harmonies of the songs their hearts and lips have sung, the breath of their souls poured out in adoration and praise, the hunger of their spirits seeking the throne of grace, the crises of their lives —great and small, strong yet tender, humble yet bold, hesitant yet pleading, self-emptying yet seeking fullness —put in the form which only those who know the love of Jesus in all of life's way can use—the very soul of prayer.

As the years have been laid away, into the

storehouse of the past have been garnered the prayers of God's saints—thousands on thousands, known and unknown, some great in name—many all but nameless, some high in life—many of humble place but great in the kingdom—a great and mighty companionship this of the pray-ers of the ages! Of the harmonies of their souls, of their humilities and glories, of their struggles and victories, of their seekings and findings, what a treasure remains!—and this is ours today.

This little book catches but the faintest trace of this mighty chorus welling through the ages—echoing, re-echoing, like a glorious antiphonal song of century singing, praying, to century, down the stretch of time; but that which herein is gathered comes from many times and many places, from many hearts, the breathings of the comings to God.

Much that is here has been found in sources away from the accustomed path of the meditating seeker; something of the inaccessible is brought close that one may make it his own; much originally breathed in tongues strange to our time and land comes garbed in the words we use, for the first time. Perhaps this has cooled the fervor or clouded over the glowing heart of the original, but still in colder tongue it remains—prayer. But

all is to serve the hunger of the heart in its
outpouring and feed the devotion of the soul
in its communion with God.

The many causes for prayer and the many
objects of prayer growing out of the many-
sided activities of the pastoral office have
guided, to a great degree, the choice and ar-
rangement of these prayers. While the hope
is to serve the pastor in his personal devotions, it will also be found that most of these
devotions are suitable for general use.

The index indicates the source of the
prayer in all but a comparatively few cases.
Quite a number of those found in the ancient
Sacramentaries have been newly translated;
while others have been quoted in the language
of the great Anglican liturgiologist, Dr.
Neale, who loved the devotional treasures of
the Church and labored so devotedly to make
them appreciated. Those found in the Kirchen
Ordnungen of the XVI Century and in other
Germanic sources, are, we believe, translated
for the first time.

SOLI DEO GLORIA. AMEN.

OREMUS

LORD, if Thou art not present, where shall I seek Thee absent? If everywhere, why do I not see Thee present? I beseech Thee, Lord, teach me to seek Thee, and show Thyself to the seeker; because I can neither seek Thee, unless Thou teach me, nor find Thee, unless Thou show Thyself to me. Let me seek Thee in desiring Thee, and desire Thee in seeking Thee: let me find Thee in loving Thee and love Thee in finding Thee.

O HEAVENLY Father, Thou dear God, I am an unworthy, miserable sinner, not worthy to lift mine eyes or hands toward Thee, or to pray; but since Thou hast commanded us all to pray and thereto hast added Thy promise to hear us, yea, even more, hast Thyself taught us both Word and Way, through Thy dear Son, our Lord JESUS CHRIST; I come to Thee, according to Thy command, obedient unto Thee, relying on Thy gracious promise; and in the Name of my Lord, JESUS CHRIST, with all Thy holy Christians on earth, I pray as He has taught me:

OUR FATHER, Who art in Heaven; Hallowed be Thy Name; Thy Kingdom come; Thy Will be done on earth as it is in Heaven; Give us this day our daily bread; And forgive us our trespasses, as we forgive those who trespass against us; And lead us not into temptation; But deliver us from evil; For Thine is the Kingdom, and the Power, and the Glory, for ever and ever. Amen.

O SACRED Heart of Jesus, filled with infinite love, broken by my ingratitude, pierced by my sins yet loving me still, accept the consecration that I make to Thee of all that I am and all that I have. Take every faculty of my soul and body, and only draw me day by day nearer and nearer to Thy sacred side, and there as I can bear the lesson teach me Thy blessed ways. Amen.

COLLECTS AND PRAYERS

BRIEF PRAYERS AND ASPIRATIONS

On awakening.

Say the *Gloria.*

THANKS be to Thee, O blessed God, for the night and its rest—for the bright'-ning day—Shine Thou upon me, Lord.

O God, Who hast given me another day of life, behold, I devote it and myself to Thee. Amen.

On rising.

IN the Name of the Father, and of the Son and of the Holy Ghost. Amen.

BLESSED be the Holy Trinity, and the un-divided Unity, Father, Son, and Holy Ghost; I confess to Him that He has kept me in His love, and commit myself to His gra-cious keeping this day. Amen.

IN the Name of our Lord, Jesus Christ, the Crucified, I arise: May He, Who has re-deemed me, keep, protect and defend me from all evil this day, always, and in the hour of my death. Amen.

I OFFER unto Thee my heart, and I pray Thee that every thought, word and deed and all my desires may be directed this day, according to Thy good pleasure. Amen.

LORD JESUS, I give Thee my body, my soul, my substance, my fame, my friends, my liberty, my life: dispose of me, and of all that is mine, as it seemeth best to Thee, and to the glory of Thy blessed Name; Who . . .

Before Divine Worship.

I WILL go into Thy House, and adore Thee in Thy sanctuary, and confess Thy Name. Accept, O Lord, my praise, the words of my mouth; but, since I am a man with unclean lips, do Thou sanctify me, and send Thy holy angel with the burning coal to cleanse my mouth, and make me worthy to Thy praise. Amen.

THEE, O good, O blessed Jesus, I wish to magnify: Intercede for me, because there is no good in me. Amen.

O LORD, take away from us all coldness, all wanderings of the thoughts, and fix our souls upon Thee and Thy love, O merciful Lord and Saviour, in this our hour of prayer. Amen.

After Divine Worship.

FORGIVE, O Lord, according to the multitude of Thy tender mercies, wherever in Thy service I have knowingly or unknowingly sinned. Amen.

GRANT, O Lord, that what we have said with our lips, we may believe in our hearts and always steadfastly fulfill. Amen.

THE Lord vouchsafe to grant that we, protected by His help, aided by His mercy, glorified by His resurrection, may with spotless minds lift up His praises in the holy Church. Amen.

On Passing or Entering a Church.

LORD, I love the habitation of Thy House, the place where Thine honor dwelleth. Lord, in the multitude of Thy tender mercies, I will enter Thy House, worship and confess Thy Name.

Before the Cross.

O CHRIST, I adore and bless Thee—through Thy Cross Thou hast redeemed the world.

We pray Thee, O Lord, that guarded by the Sign of Thy Cross, and kept safe under its guard, we may be delivered from all the snares of the devil; O Thou Who livest. . .

Before Reading Holy Scripture.

THY Word is a lamp unto my feet and a light unto my path.

My delight shall be in the law of the Lord, and in Thy law will I meditate day and night.

Lord, whither shall I go; Thou alone hast the words of eternal Life, and I believe and know that Thou art the CHRIST of God.

On Beginning any Work.

AID, direct, control me: that in Thee, with Thee, for Thee, I may do this work; because without Thee I am nothing and cannot do anything aright. Amen.

SHOW me Thy ways, O Lord, teach me Thy paths; perfect my steps in Thy ways, and let not my feet be moved therefrom.

I will follow Thee, Lord, whithersoever Thou goest—because Thou hast the words of eternal Life.

Grace before Meat.

GRANT me, Lord, Thy benediction, that I strive not for food that perisheth, but for that which remaineth in eternal Life. Amen.

MAKE me, Lord, always to hunger and thirst for righteousness; O God, my soul thirsteth for the living Water: with Thee is the Fountain of Life. Amen.

BLESS, O Lord, these Thy gifts which we are about to receive of Thy bounty. Amen.

Thanksgiving after Meat.

GLORY be to Thee, O Lord, Who hast refreshed me with food and drink; make me always to live to Thy praise. Amen.

THANKS be to God for these and all His bounties bestowed on us. Amen.

At Eventide.

O LORD, from Whom nothing is hid, with Whom there is no darkness: Send forth Thy light into my heart, that walking in Thy way, I may fall into no sin. Amen.

Before Sleep.

IN the Name of the Father, and of the Son and of the Holy Ghost. Amen.

COME Divine Love, grant me quiet sleep, that as I lay me down, trusting in Thy protecting Love, I may rest in Thee, now and in eternity. Amen.

Pillow-prayer.

GOD the Father bless me,
God the Son defend me;
God the Holy Ghost preserve me;
Now and for ever. Amen.

COLLECTS

Adoration.

O GOD, Whom to know is to live, to serve Whom is the health and joy of the soul: Thee with my lips and my heart and with all that might which I have, do I praise, bless and adore; Who livest and reignest One God, world without end. Amen.

BLESSED be God, the Only God, Three Persons in one Eternity of Love.

Blessed be God, the Lover of men, their Creator, Redeemer and Sanctifier.

Blessed be God, the Fount of human love, Whence all earthly intercourse is fructified.

Blessed be God for all that He is.

Blessed be God for all that He has done.

Blessed in His Church on earth, and blessed in the height of Heaven: blessed in the Fellowship of the Redeemed; and blessed amid all the Celestial Host; blessed by all the chorus of humanity, and blessed by the whisper of each single soul.

Blessed from everlasting, blessed now, and blessed for evermore.

Blessed be God. Amen.

TO Jesus, the Life of our flesh, Who quickeneth Whom He willeth:

To Jesus, the Life of our soul, Who came that we might live more abundantly:

To Jesus, the Life of His Church, Who loved her and gave Himself for her:

Let all in earth, and in Paradise, reconciled by His death, and saved by His life, give glory and honor, worship and praise, now and for evermore. Amen.

SPIRIT of Life, Who fillest all the world, I worship and adore Thee.

Spirit of Light, Who teachest all the Truth, I worship and adore Thee.

Source of all gifts of nature and of grace, of knowledge natural and supernatural, I worship and adore Thee.

As Thou hast made and endowed me, taught and reproved me, borne with me, recovered me, restored me; now with the ardor of a quickened soul, with the devotion of an humble mind, with the best homage of a thankful heart,

Lord and Giver-of-Life,

I worship and adore Thee. Amen.

GLORY to our Ascended Lord, that He is with us always.

Glory to the Word of God, going forth with His armies, conquering and to conquer.

Glory to Him, Who has led captivity captive, and given gifts for the perfecting of His saints.

Glory to Him Who has gone before to prepare a place in His Father's House for us.

Glory to the Author and Finisher of our faith: that God in all things may be glorified through Jesus Christ:

To Whom be all worship and praise, dominion and glory, now and for evermore. Amen.

Faith.

I BELIEVE in Thee, O God, the Father, my Maker.

I believe in Thee, O God, the Son, my Saviour.

I believe in Thee, O God, the Holy Ghost, my Helper.

Glory be to Thee, O Holy Trinity, One God. Amen.

Hope.

O MERICFUL God, in Thee is my hope; O cast not out my soul, but save it for the sake of Jesus Christ, my Lord. Amen.

Love.

I LOVE Thee, O Father, Who didst give Thy Son for me.

I love Thee, O Christ, Who on the cross didst die for me.

I love Thee, O Holy Ghost, Who didst call me, and dost sanctify me. Amen.

For Divine Aid in One's Calling.

LORD God, Thou hast placed me in Thy Church as a bishop and pastor: Thou seest how unfit I am to fulfill this great and responsible office. Had it not been for Thy wisdom and guidance, I would long since have brought everything to destruction. Therefore do I cry unto Thee. Most willingly do I desire to give and conform my mouth and heart to Thy service. I desire to teach the people; and long, continually, to be taught Thy Word. Deign to use me as Thy workman, dear Lord. Only do not Thou forsake me, for if Thou forsake me, I alone shall bring all to nought. Amen.

O GOD Almighty, the Father of Thy Only-Begotten Son: Give me a body undefiled, an heart pure, a mind watchful, an unerring knowledge, the influence of the Holy Ghost for the obtaining and the assured enjoyment of the Truth; through Thy Christ, by Whom glory be to Thee, in the Holy Ghost, unto the ages. Amen.

For Grace to do One's Work.

O GOD, Who hast commanded that no man should be idle: Give us grace to employ all our talents and faculties in the service appointed for us, that, whatsoever our hand findeth to do, we may do it with our might. Cheerfully may we go on in the road which Thou hast marked out, not desiring too earnestly that it should be either more smooth or wide; but daily, seeking our way by Thy Light, may we trust ourselves and the issue of our journey to Thee, the Fountain of Joy, and sing songs of praise as we go along. Then, O Lord, receive us at the gate of life which Thou hast opened for us in Christ Jesus, to Whom. . .

O LORD, give us the grace of Thy Spirit, early to seek out, and evermore earnestly to follow, the work which Thou hast appointed us to do; through. . .

O GOD, the Sovereign God of the soul, Who requirest the hearts of all Thy children: deliver us from all sloth in Thy work, all coldness in Thy cause; and grant us, by looking unto Thee, to rekindle our love, and by waiting upon Thee, to renew our strength; through. . .

For the Holy Ghost.

HEAVENLY King, Paraclete, Spirit of Truth, Who art everywhere present and fillest all things, the Treasury of good things and the Bestower of life: Come and dwell in us, and purify us from every stain, and save our souls, in Thy goodness; Who with the Father. . .

MAY the outpouring of the Holy Ghost, O Lord, cleanse our hearts and make them fruitful with His plenteous dew; through. . .

LET Thy mercy, O Lord, be upon us, and the brightness of Thy Spirit illumine our inward souls, that He may kindle our cold hearts and light up our dark minds, Who abideth evermore with Thee in glory.

O MERCIFUL Lord, Who understandest the groaning of the contrite heart before it is expressed, make us, we pray Thee, the temple of the Paraclete, to the end that we may be crowned with the shield of celestial mercy; through. . .

ALMIGHTY, Everlasting God, lighten our eyes with the light of Thy Spirit, that we sleep not in evil deeds, but with the help of His grace, may ever watch in Thy commandments, and, when Christ cometh, may pass to the reward of our high calling; through. . .

To Abound in Good Works.

PLANT us in Thine House, O Lord, with virtues, and make us as good seed bear fruit in all loveliness of religion, that growing up like a palm tree in the flower of righteous-ness, and perfected therein by Thee, we may flourish in joy in Thy sight for evermore; through. . .

Before Reading Holy Scripture.

O EVERLASTING God and Father of our Lord, Jesus Christ, grant me Thy grace that I may study the Holy Scriptures diligently, and, with my whole heart, seek and find Christ therein and through Him obtain everlasting life; through the same. . .

A LMIGHTY, everlasting God, Lord, Heavenly Father, Whose Word is a lamp to our feet and a light on our way: Open and enlighten my mind that I may understand Thy Word purely, clearly and devoutly, and fash-ion my life according to it, in order that I may never displease Thy Majesty; through. . .

L ORD JESUS, our King, Light and Life, illumine, waken, strengthen my heart through Thy power and Holy Word to ever-lasting life. Glory, laud and honor be unto Thee, Who with the Father and the Holy Ghost livest. . .

O GOD, with Whom is the well of life, and in Whose Light we see light: Increase in us, we beseech Thee, the brightness of

Divine knowledge, whereby we may be able to reach Thy plenteous fountain; impart to our thirsting souls the draught of life; and restore to our darkened minds the Light from Heaven; through. . .

After Reading Holy Scripture.

O GOD, Father of all mercies, Thou, Who in the unsearchable riches of Thy grace, hast opened to me the treasure of Thy Word in which we have the knowledge of Thy dear Son, and a sure pledge of our life and salvation: I beseech Thee, grant that I may preserve it in pure faith and burning love unto the end; through the Same. . .

E TERNAL Father, Gracious God, Divine Sower of Thy holy Word, Who dost grant us to be born again of this imperishable seed: We thank Thee for the treasure of Thy gospel, and humbly beseech Thee to plough our hearts with Thy law, moisten them with Thy Spirit, shine upon them with Thy Sun of Grace, so that we become good and fertile land, and bring forth much fruit in patience; through. . .

A Thanksgiving for the Holy Gospel.

W E give thanks unto Thee, Almighty God, Heavenly Father, that Thou hast given to us Thy holy gospel, and hast therein revealed to us Thy fatherly heart: We humbly beseech Thee, graciously preserve the light of Thy Word in us, and so lead and rule our hearts by Thy Holy Spirit, that we never again forsake it, but cling to its holy teaching and at last through it be saved; through. . .

Before Study.

ALMIGHTY God, our Heavenly Father, without Whose help labor is useless, without Whose light search is vain: Invigorate my studies and direct my inquiries, that I may, by due diligence and right discernment, establish myself and others in Thy holy faith; through. . .

O GOD, Who hast ordained that whatever is to be desired should be sought by labor, and Who, by Thy blessing, bringest honest labor to good effect: Look with mercy upon my studies and endeavors; grant me, O Lord, to design only what is lawful and right, and afford me calmness of mind, and steadiness of purpose, that I may so do Thy will in this short life, as to obtain happiness in the world to come; through. . .

O THOU, Who enlightenest every man who cometh into the world: Enlighten our hearts with the brightness of Thy grace, that we may ponder and love those things that are acceptable to Thee; through. . .

O LORD God, the Fountain of wisdom, Who by Thy Well-Beloved Son hast taught us that every scribe instructed unto the Kingdom of Heaven should bring forth from his treasures things old and new: Vouchsafe unto me diligence and foresight; grant me the spirit of judgment that I may discern between good and evil; the spirit of understanding that I may fully know the purport of that which I read; the gift of memory that I may retain it; and readiness with fluency, that I may use it in Thy service for the profit of souls committed to my teaching; through the Same. . .

Before Preparing a Sermon.

O GOD, the Holy Ghost, Who enlightenest the minds of Thy children: Send down upon me, I pray Thee, the spirit of wisdom and understanding to lead me into all truth, that I may so feed the flock committed to me with the words of eternal life, as with them to attain unto that place where Thou livest; Who with the Father. . .

GIVE me, O teacher, the lowliness and loftiness of mind becoming those who are thinking Thy thoughts after Thee.

O LORD and Saviour Christ, Who camest not to strive nor cry, but to let Thy words fall as the drops that water the earth: Grant all who contend for the faith once delivered, never to injure it by clamor and impatience; but speaking Thy precious truth in love, so to present it that it may be loved, and that men may see in it Thy goodness and beauty; Who livest. . .

Meditation before the Preparation of a Sermon.

L ET the preacher labor to be heard intelligently, willingly, obediently; and let him not doubt that he will accomplish this rather by the piety of his prayers than the eloquence of his speech. By praying for himself, and for those whom he is to address, let him be their beadsman before their Teacher; and approaching God with devotion, let him raise to Him a thirsting heart, before he speaks of Him with his tongue that he may speak what he hath been taught, and pour out what hath been poured in.

I cease not therefore to ask from our Lord and Master, that He may, either by the communication of His scriptures, or the conversations of my brethren, or the internal and sweeter doctrine of His own Spirit, deign to teach me things so to be proposed and asserted, that I may ever hold me fast to the Truth: from this very Truth I desire to be taught the many things I know not, and I have received the few I know. I beseech this Truth that, loving-kindness preventing and following me, He would teach me the wholesome things that I know not; keep me in the true things I know; correct me wherein I am (which is human) in error, confirm me wherein I waver; preserve me from false and noxious things and make that to proceed from my mouth which, as it shall be chiefly pleasing to the Truth Himself, so it may be accepted by all the faithful; through the Same. . .

For Illumination.

LET Thy mercy, O Lord, be upon me and the brightness of Thy Spirit illumine my inward soul; that He may kindle my cold heart, and light up my dark mind, Who abideth evermore with Thee in Glory; through

LIGHTEN our eyes, O Lord, that our faith may fix her sight upon Thee, and our soul may take counsel in the sweetness of Thy love, and Thy fear implant true penitence in our hearts; through. . .

ALMIGHTY, Everlasting God, lighten our eyes with the light of Thy Spirit, that we sleep not in evil deeds, but with the help of Thy grace, may ever watch in Thy commandments, and, when Christ cometh, may pass to the reward of our high calling in Him, through the Same. . .

GRANT, O Lord, we beseech Thee, that we may be illuminated by Thee the Light, directed by Thee the Way, corrected by Thee the Truth, quickened by Thee the Life; Who livest. . .

For Faith.

ALMIGHTY Lord God, Give us righteous, true, faith, and increase the same in us daily: give us also love and hope, in order that we may serve Thee, and our neighbor according to Thy will; through. . .

ALMIGHTY, Merciful God, we humbly beseech Thee to increase faith in us that we may walk in Thy obedience and obtain the end of faith, even the salvation of our souls; through. . .

WE beseech Thee, O Lord, in Thy compassion to increase Thy faith in us, because Thou wilt not deny the aid of Thy loving

kindness to those on whom Thou bestowest
a steadfast faith in Thee; through . .

For Hope.

MAY the hope which Thou hast given us,
O Lord, be our consolation in our low
estate, as it will fill us with glory in the day
of our rejoicing; through. . .

ALBEIT, O Lord, there be many that say
that there is no help for us in our God;
yet Thou art our Defender and the Lifter-up
of our head: Vouchsafe therefore, to give us
the increase of hope, and to surround us with
Thy perpetual mercy; through. . .

O LORD, make us ever hold fast by Thee,
and fix in Thee all the might of our
hope, that we may tell of Thy praises in the
everlasting gates; through. . .

IT is good for us, O Lord, to hold fast by
Thee; but do Thou so heap up the desire of
good in us, that the hope which joins us unto
Thee may not waver through any stumbling
of faith, but abide in the firmness of love;
through. . .

For Love.

CONFIRM, O Lord, we beseech Thee, the hearts of Thy children, and strengthen them with the power of Thy grace, that they may both be devout in prayer to Thee, and sincere in love for each other; through. . .

O GOD, Who hast enkindled in the holy bosoms of all Thy saints so great an ardor of faith, that they despised all bodily pains while hastening with all earnestness to Thee, the Author of life: Hear our prayers, and grant that the hateful sweetness of sin may wax faint in us, and that we may glow with, the infused warmth of love for Thee; through Thy mercy, O our God, Who art blessed, and dost live and govern all things, world without end.

For Heavenly Mindedness.

GRANT me, Lord, not to mind earthly things, but to love things heavenly; and even now while I am placed among things that are passing away, to cleave to those that shall abide; through. . .

For Devout Mindedness.

O LORD, with Whom is the fulness of salvation and the perfection of blessedness: Grant that we may pass our time both by day and by night in the meditation of Thy law, so that, like a fruitful tree planted by the rivers of Thy grace, we may bring forth fruit here and may be crowned with glory hereafter; through. . .

For Grace to Praise God.

O GOD, the Hope of all the ends of the earth, hearken to the humble prayer of Thy family, that while it praises Thee with tuneful harmony and the chanted hymn, it may, adorned by the inward flow of the Comforter, be enriched with abundant fruit; through. . .

O LORD Jesus Christ, by Thine excellent Name, spread through all the world by the apostles, perfect the praise of Thy victory in us who are the work of Thy hands, that our enemy may be stilled, and we be crowned with the perpetual triumph of glory and worship; Who livest. . .

GOD, Who art the only Hope of Thy servants, grant us to kindle in our meditations, that our souls may be inflamed with Thy love, and our hearts on fire with Thy praise; through. . .

CHRIST the Lord, Whose holy name is as ointment poured out: Grant, we beseech Thee, that the ointment of Thy head may be poured down by Thee, so as to descend on the beard of Thy people, and come to the very edge of the garment of this mortal life; Who livest. . .

ALMIGHTY and Holy Spirit, the Comforter pure, living, true: Illuminate, govern, sanctify me, and confirm my heart and mind in the faith, and in all genuine consolation; preserve and rule over me, that, dwelling in the house of the Lord all the days of my life, to behold the beauty of the Lord, I may be and remain forever in the temple of the Lord, and praise Him with a joyful spirit in union with all the heavenly Church; Who with the Father. . .

For Spiritual Communion.

O GOD, the Health of our countenance, after Whom the souls of Thy servants ardently long: Grant, we beseech Thee, that while we are nourished with the food of our visible tears, we may see Thee invisibly within the tabernacle of our hearts; through. . .

For Wisdom.

O GOD, Thou Who art great and terrible, Who art adorned as the glorious Prince in the heavenly Jerusalem: Expand our souls with spiritual intelligence that Thy

mercy tabernacling within our breasts, we
may be made worthy to set forth Thy Holy
Name; Who livest. . .

O GOOD Shepherd, Who, for the ransom
of Thy mortal sheep, hast drunk the cup
of the Passion: We humbly call upon Thy
Name, that, stablishing us upon the pillars of
wisdom, Thou wouldest strengthen us with the
hallowing of Thy sevenfold Spirit; Who
livest. . .

O GOD, the Searcher of deeds and hearts,
to Whom every thought of man maketh
confession: Strengthen the weakness of our
minds by the might of Thy blessing, that we
may think such things as be just and holy,
and by a good life pay our faithful vows to
Thee, our Lord God; through. . .

To Pray Aright.

O LORD, I beseech Thee to look upon
Thy servant, whom Thou hast enabled
to put his trust in Thee; and grant him both
to ask such things as shall please Thee, and
through Thy love, obtain the same; through. . .

O LORD, Who seest that all hearts are
empty except Thou fill them, and all desires balked except they crave after Thee:

Give us light and grace to seek and find Thee, that we may be Thine and Thou mayest be ours forever; through. . .

For the Spirit of Prayer.

O GOD of hope, the true Light of faithful souls, and perfect Brightness of the blessed, Who art verily the Light of the Church: Grant that my heart may both render Thee a worthy prayer, and always glorify Thee with the offering of praise; through...

For Growth in Grace.

O GOD, Who in Thy loving kindness dost both begin and finish all good things: Grant that as we glory in the beginnings of Thy grace, so we may rejoice in its completion; through. . .

To Love Righteousness.

GRANT, Lord, that we may love righteousness and hate iniquity, so that, advancing by Thee the Way, to Thee the End, we may be led by Thy wonderful right hand to the kingdom of eternal beauty; Who livest...

For Consecration.

O HOLY Spirit, Love of God, infuse Thy grace, and descend plentifully into my heart; enlighten the dark corners of this neglected dwelling, and scatter there Thy brightening beams; dwell in that soul that longs to be Thy temple; water that barren soil, overrun with weeds and briars, and lost for want of cultivating, and make it fruitful with Thy dew from heaven. O come Thou Refreshment of them that languish and faint. Come Thou Star and Guide of them that sail in the tempestuous sea of the world; Thou only Haven of the tossed and ship-wrecked. Come Thou Glory and Crown of the living, and only Safeguard of the dying. Come, Holy Spirit, in much mercy, and make me fit to receive Thee, Who with the Father...

CAUSE us, O Lord, to become heirs of Thy testimonies, which have been made matter of belief unto us, let them be constantly in our thought, that they may be sincerely held in true faith, and be so fulfilled in our work, that as they are uttered by the mouth they may guide us in sorrow with their comfort, and make us more ready to labor with Thee; through...

LORD, do Thou turn me all into love, and all my love into obedience, and let my obedience be without interruption; and then I hope Thou wilt accept such a return as I

can make. Make me to be something that
Thou delightest in, and Thou shalt have all
that I am or have from Thee, even whatsoever Thou makest for Thyself; through. . .

L IVING or dying, Lord, I would be Thine:
Keep me Thine forever, and draw me
day by day nearer to Thyself, until I be
wholly filled with Thy love, and fitted to behold Thee face to face; through. . .

Self-Surrender.

L ORD, take my lips, and speak through
them; take my mind, and think through
it; take my heart, and set it on fire; through

To do God's Will.

O GOOD Jesus, Word of the Father,
Splendor of the Father's glory, on
Whom the angels desire to gaze; Teach me
to do Thy will, that led by Thy good Spirit
I may reach that blessed City where is eternal
day, and One Spirit amongst all, where is
certain safety, and safe eternity, and eternal
peace and peaceful happiness, and happy
sweetness and sweet enjoyment, where Thou
livest. . .

For Purity of Heart.

O GOD, who lovest all that is sincere and pure, and dwellest of Thy bountiful goodness in the chaste souls of the faithful: Purify us from all taint of sin, that we may always have our heart ready for Thee, and sing and play worthily unto Thee in Thy glory; through. . .

To Abound in Works of Mercy.

O CHRIST, our God, make us ever ready to aid the poor and needy, and to keep Thy law, that abounding in works of mercy, we may become the fellows of the heavenly citizens; Who livest. . .

For Godly Life.

M AKE us, O Lord, to flourish like pure lilies in the courts of Thine House, and to show forth to the faithful the fragrance of good works, and the example of a godly life; through. . .

For Grace to Use One's Gifts.

O LORD God of righteousness, Who art ever merciful and lendest: So bestow on Thy servants the talents which Thou seest to be expedient for them, that they may return them with a good increase to Thy glory and honor; Who livest. . .

For Divine Guidance and Protection.

GRANT us, O Lord, we beseech Thee, always to seek Thy kingdom and righteousness; and of whatsoever Thou seest us to stand in need, mercifully grant us an abundant portion. . .

GRANT, we beseech Thee, Almighty God, unto us who know that we are weak and who trust in Thee because we know that Thou art strong, the gladsome help of Thy loving kindness, both here in time and hereafter in eternity; through. . .

O LORD, Keeper of the faithful, ever preserve and keep us from the generation of the ungodly, and unite us to the generation of the righteous who keep Thy pure words, that we may always abide in Thy love, and by the help of Thine aid, rejoice in everlasting salvation; through. . .

SHOW Thy marvelous loving kindness, O Lord, hide us under the shadow of Thy wings, keep us as the apple of Thine eye, that our goings may be perfected in Thy paths; and we may appear with Thee in righteousness and be satisfied when Thy glory shall appear; through. . .

O OUR King and God, lead us in Thy righteousness because of our enemies, and direct our way in Thy sight, that Thou mayest ever rejoice and dwell in us who art crowned with the shield of Thy good will; through. . .

CONSIDER and hear us, O Lord: assist our timid efforts, give the end of the act, Thou Who didst give the beginning of the will: grant that we may be able to accomplish the thing which Thou hast already granted that we should desire to commence; through. .

O LORD Jesus Christ, Wisdom of God the Father, give us understanding and inform us with Thy precepts, guide us with Thine eye in the way we go, that under Thy leading we may surely come to Thee, Who art the Way, the Truth and the Life; Who livest. . .

OPEN, O Merciful Lord, Thy ears to our prayers, Thou Who never failest them who trust in Thee: so that we, being lifted up from the gates of perpetual death, may be able safely to escape the snares of the tempter; through. . .

OF Thy merciful goodness, O Lord, attend to the desire of the poor, and bestow on us the abundance of Thy celestial gifts; remove from us the love of the passing things of this world, and since Thou defendest the humble and the orphan, give us the joy of Thy fatherly mercy: bestowing for the humiliation of this world, the joys of the Kingdom of Heaven; through. . .

WE beseech Thee, O Lord, to preserve us unhurt from the works of anti-Christ, to the end, that we, deserting him and acknowledging Christ the Lord as our Father, may follow Thee by our faith, may retain Thee by our love, may glorify Thee by our good works; through the Same. . .

Before a Journey.

O GOD, Who didst cause the children of Israel to pass dry-shod through the midst of the sea, and Who, by the leading of a star didst open to the Magi the way unto Thyself: Grant to us, we beseech Thee, a prosperous journey and fair weather; that attended by Thy holy Angel, we may happily arrive at that place whither we are going, and finally attain to the haven of eternal salvation; through. . .

O GOD, Who didst bring Abraham, Thy son, out of Ur of the Chaldees, and didst preserve him unhurt through all the ways of his pilgrimage: We beseech Thee, that Thou wouldest vouchsafe to keep us Thy servants: be unto us, O Lord, support in our setting out, comfort by the way, a shadow in the heat, a covering in the rain and cold, a chariot in weariness, protection in adversity, a staff in slippery ways and a harbor in shipwreck: that under Thy guidance we may reach in prosperity the place whither we are going and at length return to our home in safety; through. . .

ASSIST us mercifully, O Lord, in these our supplications and prayers, and dispose the way of Thy servants towards the attainment of everlasting salvation that among all the changes and chances of this mortal life, we may ever be defended by Thy most gracious and ready help; through. . .

GRANT, we beseech Thee, Almighty God, that Thy family may walk in the way of salvation, and, by following the counsels of St. John the Forerunner, may come in safety unto Him, Whom he preached, Thy Son, Jesus Christ, our Lord, Who. . .

After a Safe Return.

ALMIGHTY, everlasting God, Who order- est all our days, and all our life: Grant unto Thy servants the gifts of continual peace; and as Thou hast brought us back again in safety to our home, do Thou ever preserve us in quietness under Thy protec- tion; through. . .

For Angelic Guard.

O GOD, Who in Thy unspeakable prov- idence dost vouchsafe to send Thy holy angels to be our guard: Grant that we, Thy humble servants, may always be defended by their aid and rejoice in their everlasting fel- lowship; through. . .

For Meekness.

ALMIGHTY and everlasting God, grant that our wills be ever meekly subject to Thy will, and our hearts be ever honestly ready to serve Thee; through. . .

O GOD, mercifully grant us that the fire of Thy love may burn up in us all things that displease Thee, and make us meet for Thy heavenly Kingdom; through. . .

Against Pride.

O LORD MOST HIGH, Who beholdest the lowly, grant us lowliness that we may please Thee, nor suffer pride to remain within us, which Thou throwest afar off and destroyest when near: that, of Thy mercy, the haughtiness which casteth down may depart from our mind, and contrition which bringeth glory may abide in our heart; through. . .

To Rejoice in Other Men's Success.

A LMIGHTY God, give me the power and grace to rejoice over other men's brightness and strength and success; through Him Who laid down His life for His friends, our Master Jesus Christ. . .

Against a Froward Heart.

W E sing of mercy and judgment unto Thee, O Lord, our Saviour and Judge, help us with the one, warn us with the other; on that side is the light of pity, on this the rule of inquiry; grant us Thy humble servants, O Lord, that a froward heart may not cleave to us, and that evil things before our eyes may not allure us; but that walking in the simplicity of innocence, Thou mayest lead us on in Thy pity and love, and absolve us as a truthful Judge; Who livest. . .

For Obedience.

MAKE us of quick and tender conscience, O Lord; that understanding, we may obey every word of Thine, and discerning, may follow every suggestion of Thine indwelling Spirit; through. . .

For Prudence.

LET wisdom, we beseech Thee, O Lord, open our mouth, and let prudence dwell on our tongue: and to the end we may not be compared to the beasts that perish, instruct us in the discipline of Thy Divine laws, that so our understanding may comprehend Thee on earth, and may enjoy Thee for ever in heaven; through. . .

For Control of One's Tongue.

O CHRIST, Son of the living God, Who for our sakes wast made the Bread of the universe: Grant that we may never be led away by the temptation of our enemy, but may follow Thee in the true government of our tongue; through the Same. . .

ALMIGHTY God, Who settest men's minds upon righteousness, and causest them to judge the thing that is right: Grant that there may be neither evil on our lips, nor iniquity in our hearts; so that righteousness in works may precede good speaking in tongue; through. . .

LET our lips be firm in Thee, O Lord, with the tidings of Truth, that they may never be loosed in the vain speech of error; and may ever speak Thy glory and may never cry aloud in the unseemly disputes of quarrelling; that as Thy martyr and forerunner, John the Baptist, did unswervingly herald Thy coming, so we may ever speak to Thy praise; Who livest. . .

WE beseech Thee, O Lord, that our human mouth being filled with Thy praise, we may ever think in our hearts of that which we offer Thee with acceptable voices; through. . .

O LORD, Most High, be Thou our Helper, and make haste with speed to deliver Thy people, that by Thine abundant power we may be filled with mighty help, and be enriched with gifts from the bounty of Thine abundant grace, that our tongue may not be-

come slow through falsehood when we pro-
fess love to Thee with our mouth, but let that
profession of our mouth denote purity of
mind, and let Thy praise ever sound on our
lips from the organ of the heart; through...

Tongue and Lips.

WE beseech Thee, O Lord, that Thou
wouldest keep our tongues from evil
and our lips from speaking guile; that as Thy
holy angels ever sing praises to Thee in
heaven, so with our tongues we may at all
times glorify Thee on earth; through. . .

Temper and Tongue.

O LORD, our Refuge from the storm, hide
us, we entreat Thee, in Thine Own
presence from the provoking of all men; and
by Thy holy love and fear keep us from
sins of temper and tongue; through. . .

Secret Sins.

A LMIGHTY, Eternal God, through Whom
that which is not beginneth to be, and
that which is hidden is made manifest:
Cleanse the folly of our hearts and purify us
of those vices which are secret, so that we
may be able to serve Thee, O Lord, with a
pure mind; through. . .

For Deliverance from Temptation.

O LORD, I beseech Thee to renew me inwardly and outwardly, that as Thou wouldest not have me to be hindered by bodily pleasures, Thou mayest make me vigorous with spiritual purpose; and refresh me according to Thy pleasure by things transitory, that Thou mayest grant me rather to cling to things eternal; through. . .

O LORD, my Support and Refuge, deliver me from temptation, give me the defence of Thy salvation, hold me up with Thy right hand, teach me by Thy discipline, and make my way and my life undefiled; through. . .

For Victory in Temptation.

O GOD, the Might of all them that put their trust in Thee : Grant that we may be more than conquerors over all that make war upon our souls, and in the end may enter into perfect peace in Thy presence; through. . .

O THOU, Who in the wilderness didst pass through the deepest woes of temptation, Who callest the weary, heavy-laden and sore-beset unto Thee, and Who through Thy blessed apostle comfortest those who are tried with the assurance that with Thy help, the temptation may be endured and safely passed: Be present to my great need, and graciously carry me safely through this hour; Who with. . .

ALMIGHTY God, the Preserver of Thy people in their invisible wars, Who permittest not them that put their trust in Thee to be oppressed by their enemies: Wipe away, we beseech Thee, the tears of sin from the eyes of Thy servants, to the end that we through Thy grace may both now conquer in every carnal battle, and walk before Thee in the Light of the living; through. . .

O GOD, Who hast willed that Thy saints should be tried on earth by Thy wonted loving probation, but not that they should be tempted above the gift of endurance which Thou grantest them of Thy bounty: Deliver us from all temptation, lest it overcome our mind, that serving Thee faithfully in well pleasing obedience, Thou wouldest suffer us to be so tried that temptation lead us not into the confusion of error, but bind us firmly in the embrace of Truth; through. . .

For Renewal.

WE have walked long enough, O Lord, according to the old man, give us grace to be renewed daily according to the grace of the Holy Spirit, that we may so watch over our words, and reckon our deeds, that we may finally come to Everlasting Life; through. . .

In Trouble.

WE call on Thee, O Lord, in the day of our trouble, that Thou wouldest give us the increase of faith and hope, to the end that we may come to the everlasting inheritance of love; through. . .

In Adversity.

REDEEM, O Lord, the souls of Thy servants, who put their trust in Thee; grant of Thy clemency that we may find Thy blessing in adversity as well as in prosperity; and, because Thou art nigh to them that are of a contrite heart, open Thine ears to the spirit of our sorrow and need, and let Thy peace, which passeth all understanding, keep our souls and bodies; through. . .

O GOD, be Thou to us in adversity Refuge, in battle Consolation, to the end that when Thou shalt come to judge the earth, they may be sharers with Thee in joy, who have been followers after Thee in sorrow; through. . .

O GOD, the Father of the Only-Begotten Son, Who dwellest in heaven, and Who turnest to derision those who rise up against Thy Christ: Give us this special grace, that we may never yield to adversities, to the end that the unbelief of them that know Thee not may be confounded, and the faith of them that cling to Thee may be crowned; through the Same. . .

O LORD, those are increased that trouble us: Let Thy mercy be increased above them, for then we shall fear no evil, when we are defended by Thy Grace; through. . .

ALMIGHTY, Everlasting God, FATHER Who, in Thy paternal goodness, placest us, Thy children, here on earth, under the cross, and permittest all manner of tempests to beat upon us, thereby to restrain sin and turn us to repentance, faith, hope and earnest prayer: We beseech Thee to comfort us through Thy Holy Spirit in all our tribulation and need, hear our prayer, and graciously provide help, so that we do not despair but confess Thy Fatherly grace and Presence, and

with all Thy saints, laud, worship and thank
Thee in eternity; through. . .

In Suffering.

O THOU, Who chastenest whom Thou
lovest, grant us grace, we pray Thee,
to discern Thy love in whatever suffering
Thou sendest us; support us in patient thankfulness under pain, anxiety, or loss, and move
us with pity and tenderness for our afflicted
neighbors; through. . .

O GOD, Whose eyes regard Him Who for
our sakes was poor: Be the Succorer of
the heart that putteth its trust in Thee: and
like as we do desire to be healed by the wounds
of His Passion, grant that we may be delivered in all the dangers of our own; through
the Same. . .

For Strength to Suffer and Persevere.

O LORD, let that become possible to me
by Thy grace, which by nature seems
impossible to me. Thou knowest that I am
able to suffer but little, and that I am quickly
cast down when a slight adversity ariseth:
for Thy Name's sake, let every exercise of
tribulation be amiable and desirable to me;
for to suffer and to be disquieted for Thy

sake is very wholesome for my soul; Who
livest. . .

In Cross Bearing.

O LORD, what cross willest Thou that I
should bear this day for love of Thee?
Thou knowest, Lord, that I am all weakness;
strengthen me to bear it patiently, humbly,
lovingly. If I sink under it, look upon me
and raise me up. Give what Thou commandest and command what Thou wilt; sanctify
my cross to me, and keep me Thine own
forever; Who livest. . .

In Danger.

GRANT, we beseech Thee, Almighty God,
that we, who in our tribulation are yet
of good cheer because of Thy loving kindness, may find Thee mighty to save from all
dangers; through. . .

In Persecution.

GOD, Who searchest the heart and triest
the reins, deliver us from them that per-
secute us; and grant us, through the expectation of Thy judgment, such firm trust of heart
that we may never recompense to our enemies
evil for evil; through. . .

In Deep Distress.

O LORD, let Thy mercy speedily go before us, for there is neither comforting hope, nor trust in merit, nor helpful assistance to support us; but the guilt and trouble of our life, the consciousness of our sins, or the vengeance on our offences rebukes us in our sins for Thy name's sake, that when Thou hast done both for Thyself, and hast looked on Thy people with Thy wonted loving kindness, we may give Thee glory for Thy deliverance; through Thy mercy. . .

O LORD, Who didst of old time suffer in our body, when wilt Thou look upon us? When wilt Thou turn the eyes of Thy clemency to our groans and distress? Delay not, tarry not, now draw nigh; now be Thou turned to us; now regard us, that our prayer, which now, by reason of our secret sins, returns back again into our own bosom, may, by the abundance of Thy mercy, enter into Thy presence, and be accepted by Thee. Amen. Through Thy mercy, Who livest. . .

Against Despair.

A LMIGHTY God, although our iniquities have offended Thee: Grant that our prayers and our confession may obtain Thy mercy, that through Thy loving kindness, no tribulation of this world may cause us to despair, no harmful persuasion may allure us to evil; but that the light of Thy countenance may shine upon us, and that from Thy light in this world, we may come to the light of Thine everlasting vision; through. . .

For Hope amid Tribulation.

HEAR us, we beseech Thee, O Lord, and have mercy upon us in our tribulations; and as Thou alone art glorious over the people, give spiritual joy to us, who look for the hope of Thine eternal rewards; through. . .

To Rejoice in God's Will Toward Us.

O GOD, Who chastisest us in Thy love, and refreshest us amid Thy chastening: Grant that we may ever be able to give Thee thanks for both; through. . .

For Constancy.

O GOD, incomprehensible, Who doest great wonders, Who changest the waters, which once stood still in Thy sight, at later time into wine: We humbly beseech Thee to hear the voice of our crying, to bestow on us such remembrance that we may never forget Thee; Who livest. . .

For Repentance.

ALMIGHTY and Most Merciful God, Who didst bring forth a fount of living water for Thy thirsting people out of the rock: Bring forth tears of repentance from our hard hearts, that we may be enabled to bewail our sins, and through Thy mercy obtain forgiveness; through. . .

WE know, O Lord Jesus Christ, that whilst Thou wast on earth, Thou didst every night water Thy couch with tears for us men: Grant us so to repent for our iniquities, that we may hereafter come to that place where all tears are wiped from all eyes: Who livest. . .

O CHRIST, Son of the Living God, Whose beauty in Thy Passion departed for very heaviness and has worn away because of all Thine enemies: Heal the wounds of our hearts, that Thy grace being confirmed in us, we may so put our trust in Thy Passion as to find our glory in Thy Resurrection; Who livest. . .

For Forgiveness.

CLEANSE us, O Lord, from our secret faults, by purifying our conscience which is stained with its own defilements; set free Thy servants also from the dominion of their enemies, and forgive us those things which we have learned by the example of the wicked or have done through the persuasion of evil counsellors; that we, who confess Thee to be our own Lord, may never again experience the domination of sin; through. . .

WE beseech Thee, O Lord God, to hide Thy face from our sins, and to forgive all our misdeeds, and as the publican who stood afar off was heard for the sake of his humility, so hear us for the merits of our humility, of Him, Who being co-equal with Thee, His Father, yet for our sakes vouchsafed to take upon Him the form of a servant, even our Lord Jesus Christ; Who liveth

HEAR us when we call, O Lord Jesus Christ, Who art our Righteousness; that as Thou didst for the wicked undergo all miseries, so Thou wouldest on the penitent bestow all mercies; Who livest. . .

O LORD, the Expectation of our salvation: Receive the prayers of them that call upon Thee; Thou that art the Discoverer of hidden things, give ear to the hidden cry of the heart, that those things which we tremble to have committed and blush to confess, Thou, our King, mayest forgive of Thy clemency, and blot out of Thy goodness; so that our supplication may rise to Thee in the morning, and the good gifts of Thy mercy may descend on us right early; through. . .

WE have sinned, O Lord, we confess, like prodigal sons; we dare not look up to heaven: for it was thence we fell and became wretched; we have sinned against heaven and before Thee, and we are not worthy to be called Thy sons, we denounce ourselves, we need neither accusers nor witnesses, we have iniquity triumphing over us, we have evil conversation condemning us: Merciful Father, Only-Begotten Son, Holy Ghost, receive us penitent, and have mercy upon us. Amen.

After Receiving Absolution.

ALMIGHTY, Everlasting God, we have sinned against Thee in many ways and for these our sins have justly deserved eternal condemnation, but since we believe Thy dear Son, our Lord, Jesus Christ, has

obtained with Thee the forgiveness of sins
and everlasting salvation for us, and we, but
now, have been made confident of the same
through the Holy Gospel and absolution: we
beseech Thee right humbly and obediently, to
endow us with the power of Thy Holy Spirit
in order that we may guard ourselves hereafter against sin and live a true and godly life
in Thy service; through the Same. . .

L ORD Jesus, Whose wonderful Name the
Angel foretold, Thy mother bestowed,
Simeon acknowledged, Anna praised: Save
Thy people in all the world, Thou whose name
is majestic in heaven, that Thou Who only
art glorious in power, mayest also be gentle in
Thy merciful pardon to the lost; Who livest. . .

For Peace.

O GOD, our Refuge and Strength, be present with us in all our troubles, that
every adverse sword may be sheathed and
every heart may be enriched with the blessings of peace; so that in tranquillity we may
behold Thee, and beholding Thee may possess
Thee forever; through. . .

V OUCHSAFE, O Lord, to look down from
Thy holy heaven upon the children of
men, and give us to know the way of peace;

that we, being set free from the hard captivity of vice, may enjoy the habitations of
the heavenly Jerusalem; through. . .

O GOD, Who art Peace everlasting, Whose
chosen reward is the gift of peace, and
Who hast taught us that the peacemakers are
Thy children: Pour Thy peace into our souls,
that everything discordant may utterly vanish,
and all that makes for peace be sweet to us
forever; through. . .

O GOD, Who hast taught us to keep all Thy
heavenly commandments by loving Thee
and our neighbor: Grant us the Spirit of peace
and grace, that we may be both devoted to
Thee with our whole heart, and united to each
other with a pure will; through. . .

That One's Prayer be Heard.

O CHRIST, Who didst exclaim from the
cross to the Father, "My God, My God,
why hast Thou forsaken me?"—Who by Thy
cross didst redeem lost man, and didst give
Satan to be bound in eternal chains: We beseech Thy mercy, that Thou wouldst never
forsake us who believe in Thee, never repel us
who confide in Thee; but that when we cry in
the day-time Thou wouldest hear, and in the

night-season also Thou wouldest receive our prayer; Who livest. . .

Thanksgiving for Heard Prayer.

O GOD, Whose mercy is limitless, Who art an inexhaustible Fount of blessings: We give Thy Majesty praise and thanksgiving for all the gifts which Thou hast bestowed upon us; and we beseech Thy mercy, that, from those whose prayer Thou hast granted, Thou wilt not in the future withhold Thy help, but make them fit to the attaining of the Future Blessing; through. . .

O LORD, we beseech Thee, graciously receive our prayers and supplications which we bring before Thee with thanksgiving, and grant that we, whom Thou in grace hast heard, may be genuinely thankful to Thee, praise and magnify Thy holy name and ever increase in Thy love and service; through. . .

For Contentment.

GRANT, O Lord, that Thy servants, devoted to Thy service, and confiding in Thy protection, may obtain the blessing which they humbly implore; that being at rest under Thy defence, they may not be left destitute of assistance for this life, and may be prepared for the good things which are eternal; through. . .

ALMIGHTY God, our Heavenly Father, Who dost feed the birds and clothe the flowers, and carest for us as a father for his children: We beseech Thee, graciously guard us against distrust and vain over-carefulness, and help us, through Thy Holy Spirit, to live to the hallowing of Thy name, the coming of Thy Kingdom and the doing of Thy will, so that we may cast all our care on Thee and in unwavering faith abide trustingly in Thee; through. . .

FOR THE CHURCH

General.

VISIT, O Lord, this Vine, which Thou hast brought out of the Egypt of troubles with Thy strong right hand; that quickened by the light of Thy countenance, it may be glad with the plenteousness of good fruits in Thee; through. . .

ALMIGHTY God, Who hast sent Thine Only-Begotten Son, and hast revealed Him as Creator of all things, look upon this Vine, which Thy right hand hath planted, prune away the thorns from it, bring forth its branches in might, and give them the fruit of truth; through. . .

O GOD, Whose throne endureth forever: Grant that Thy Church may be enriched by the excellent beauty of all virtues; while, nevertheless, she is far more glorious, through the indwelling of Thy ever-present Spirit; Who livest. . .

O CHRIST, the Word of the Father, by Whom all things were created: Keep, we beseech Thee, Thy Church gathered together from the various nations of the Gentiles: that while we love Thee with a pure heart, we may come to the joys of Thine eternal Kingdom; Who livest. . .

O THOU Who art great and highly to be praised: Spread abroad the faith of Thy Church into all realms, to the end, that as in all its degrees Thou art acknowledged to be GOD, Thou mayest also be praised in the united devotion of her members; receive of Thy mercy, her prayers, and in the midst of the tempests of this world, be Thou her watchful Pilot, so that we may by Thy mercy enter that City which Thou hast founded for ever and ever, and may be received therein, and may tell within its towers Thy marvelous works; through. . .

In Time of Trial.

LET the sorrows and woes of Thy suffering Church come before Thee, O Lord Jesus Christ, and as Thou hast promised to be with her always, even unto the end of the world, hallow the trials by Thy loving, strengthening presence and strengthen her to endure affliction faithfully, enable her to carry her cross after Thee and to be faithful even unto death that she may come to the glory which Thou wilt reveal, where Thou livest...

For the Parish Church.

ALMIGHTY and everlasting God, Whom the heaven of heavens cannot contain, yet Who art willing to have an house fashioned by man, wherein Thine honor dwelleth and where men may worship Thee: Of Thy love and mercy, we beseech Thee, vouchsafe Thy presence here that this Church which we have reared to the glory of Thy name, may by Thee be accepted and hallowed, to the end that souls may here be gathered, nourished in Thy love, and made fruitful in Thy service; through. . .

ALMIGHTY and everlasting God, Who callest men to the service of Thy sanctuary: Vouchsafe to all who here minister before Thee the direction, aid and counsel of Thy Holy Spirit, that they may serve Thee with pure hearts and holy lives; preach Thy Word according to Thy loving purpose in Christ Jesus; humbly and devoutly administer Thy sacraments; and be found acceptable to Thee as good and faithful stewards of Thy grace; through. . .

MOST Merciful Father, Who hast revealed Thy love in Jesus Christ, Thy dear Son, and through Thy Holy Word dost announce the precious message of salvation in Him:

Vouchsafe Thy love to all who hear Thy Word read and preached in this place, that, called to Thy service, they may hold fast the truth, and faithfully bear, unto the end, the yoke of Jesus Christ, Thy dear Son, our Lord.

ALMIGHTY God, Heavenly Father, Who through the washing of regeneration by water and the Word, hast ordained a sacramental means of entrance into Thy Kingdom: Vouchsafe to all who shall be consecrated to Thee in this font in holy baptism, ever to remain true to this blessed covenant, and finally to attain everlasting life; through. . .

MOST Merciful Father, Who in Thy dear Son hast given us the Way, the Truth, and the Life, and through Him dost call all men to give Thee heart and soul and strength and life: Vouchsafe to all who, here before this altar, confess the Lord Jesus before men, the blessing of Thy Holy Spirit, that in Thy Church they may be living stones, elect and precious; through. . .

ALMIGHTY God, Everlasting Father, Who dost refresh us as we have need, and dost strengthen our faith with heavenly food, so that we go from strength to strength: Vouchsafe to all who receive at this altar the holy sacrament of the body and blood of Thy dear Son, to approach this holy mystery with pure hearts, believing desire, and devout thanksgiving, that, comforted with Thy eternal love and goodness, they may be nourished and strengthened in faith, live in love and to the praise of Thy holy name, and finally attain to Thy presence in eternity; through. . .

O GOD, Who dost call all men to Thee, and Who dost graciously receive all them that come: Vouchsafe Thy pardon to all those who here confess their sins; bestow the comfort of Thy Spirit on those who humbly and faithfully bring Thee their needs and sorrows; accept the praise and worship that are offered here; and grant that many may find Thee in this place, and finding Thee, be filled in soul and body with all things needful; and finally, with all Thine own, be united in that communion with Thee which is eternal in the heavens, where Thou livest and reignest, ever One God, world without end. Amen.

For the Propagation of the Gospel.

O MOST Glorious Lord, magnify the joys of all the earth, to the end that faith, being spread abroad, it may fill the whole world, and that, according to the glory of

Thy name, Thou mightest enable us to glorify
Thy praise; through. . .

For Christian Unity.

O GOD our Father, Good beyond all that
is good, Fair beyond all that is fair, in
Whom is calmness and peace: Do Thou make
up the dissensions which divide us from each
other, and bring us back into a unity of love,
which may bear some likeness to Thy sub-
lime nature; grant that we may be spiritually
one, as well in ourselves as in each other,
through that peace of Thine which maketh
all things peaceful, and through the grace,
mercy and tenderness of Thy Son, Who. . .

For the Ministry.

JESUS, our God, Who, making a whip of
small cords, dravest out those who bought
and sold in Thy temple: Grant to us in Thy
Church not to be taken with the gain of tem-
poral things, nor to dwell within it in evil
conversation: but that the zeal of Thy house
may so eat us up, that Thou wouldst make of
us examples for the brethren, pleasing unto
Thee; Who livest. . .

O HOLY Lord, Father almighty, eternal
God, carry onward in us the gifts of Thy
grace, and mercifully bestow by Thy Spirit

what human frailty cannot attain, that they
who minister before Thee may be both
grounded in perfect faith, and conspicuous by
the brightness of their souls; through. . .

For Men for the Ministry.

O LORD, we beseech Thee, to raise up for
the work of the ministry faithful and
able men, counting it all joy to spend and be
spent for the sake of Thy dear Son, and for
the souls for which He shed His most precious
blood upon the cross; and we pray Thee to fit
them for their holy function by Thy bountiful
grace and benediction; through the Same. . .

For Those about to be Ordained.

O LORD, our God, Who by Thine own
presence dost shed the abundance of
Thy Holy Spirit on those who are set apart,
by Thine inscrutable power, to become ministers and to serve Thee: Keep Thy servants
who are (this day) to be ordained to the
office of the holy ministry, that they may hold
the mystery of the faith in a pure conscience
with all virtue; vouchsafe them Thy grace,
enable them to administer according to Thy
good pleasure; and fill them by the power of
Thy all-holy and life-giving Spirit with all
faith and love and power and sanctification;

for Thou art our God, and to Thee we render glory; through. . .

For the Anniversary of Ordination.

O GOD, by Whose command the order of all time runs its course: Look graciously upon me Thy servant, whom Thou hast been pleased to call to Thy service, and that my service may be pleasing unto Thee, do Thou mercifully preserve in me Thy gifts; through. . .

For Synod.

E NLIGHTEN us, we beseech Thee, O God, with the gifts of the Holy Ghost; enrich us with the power of Thy holy Word; unite us in the love and peace of Christ; guard us, we implore Thee, from the snares of sin, the temptations of the world, the weaknesses of our own nature; rule us to the fulfilling of Thy holy mysteries; direct all our ways to the advancement of Thy Church; abide with us and keep us ever in Thee, O Thou our God; through. . .

O ALMIGHTY and Everlasting God, Who hast given the Comforter to Thy Church, that He should abide with it forever: Pour forth the blessing of Thy Spirit on our pastors now assembled . . . (about to assemble) . . . in Thy name: defend their hearts from all hindrances of this world, and from all earthly feeling; grant them abundantly, steadfastness of faith, purity of love, sincere desire for peace, and firmness of authority, that they, by the help of Thy Son Jesus Christ our Lord, may both rule Thy flock committed to their care, according to Thy will, and also, together with their people, receive from the great Shepherd and Bishop of us all the rewards which are promised to Thy saints, and be united to the number of Thine elect; through the Same. . .

For Missionaries.

O LORD Jesus Christ, Who ascending to Thy throne of glory didst leave as heritage to Thy disciples the transcending privilege of carrying the banner of Thy victory and the message of Thy love to every people: As Thou hast promised to be with Thine own unto the end, vouchsafe Thy strenghtening presence to all those who have gone forth in Thy name to strange lands and peoples; enable them by Thy Spirit to preach, teach, and live Thee in all Thy love and tenderness, granting them in the ingathering of souls that inspiration of joy that shall make them strong to persevere, and to carry their cross in carrying Thine; Who. . .

O LORD, make ready the way in the dark lands, in the hearts which know Thee not; that those who, consecrated to the fulfilling of Thy last command, are carrying the message of the cross to the souls of men, may, constantly aided and uplifted by Thee, labor to the enriching of Thy great harvest; Who. . .

For Confirmands.

O GOD, Whose Spirit multiplies and rules the whole body of the Church, conserve in those who have dedicated themselves to Thy service, the grace of sanctification, which Thou alone dost impart; so that, renewed in body and mind, they may serve Thee zealously in the unity of the faith; through. . .

For the Ministry of Mercy.

MOST MERCIFUL FATHER, Who dost commit to our love and care our fellowmen in their necessities: Graciously be with and prosper all those who are seeking and ministering to the sick and needy; let their ministry be abundantly blessed in bringing ease to the suffering, comfort to the sorrowing, and peace to the dying; and themselves be inspired with the consecration to selfless service, knowing that inasmuch as they do it unto the least of the Master's brethren, they do it unto Him; through Him Who came to minister Thy Love unto men, even Jesus Christ, Thy Son. . .

FOR FAMILY AND FRIENDS

General.

ALMIGHTY and Everlasting God, be Thou present to our duties, and grant the protection of Thy presence to all that dwell in this house, that Thou mayest be known to be the Defender of Thy family, and the Inhabitant of this dwelling; through. . .

WE beseech Thee, O Lord, make Thy servants always to join together in seeking Thee with their whole heart, to serve Thee with submissive mind, humbly to implore Thy mercy, and perpetually to rejoice in Thy blessings; through. . .

O ALMIGHTY God, look graciously upon this household gathered together in Thy name: Give them whom Thou hast set over it wisdom to direct those committed to their charge; give to its members strength to fulfill Thy will in the daily work to which Thou hast appointed them; grant that love and peace, with all other graces, may live and grow among us; and that finally we may meet before Thy throne in heaven, and be united in Thy love forever; through. . .

BLESS, O God, all the members of this family (especially those who are absent from us); preserve them waking; guard them sleeping; that while they wake they may watch with Christ, and when they sleep they may rest in peace; through. . .

For One's Parents.

ALMIGHTY God, Who hast strictly commanded us to honor our father and our mother next unto Thee: Grant me of Thy goodness and grace so to love and honor my parents, to fear and to obey them, to help and to pray for them, as Thou in Thy Holy Word hast directed and charged me to do; that both in their life and at their death their souls may bless me, and by Thy fatherly mercy I may obtain that blessing which Thou hast promised to those that honor their father and their mother; and that Thou, seeing my unfeigned heart and reverence toward them, mayest become my loving Father, and number me among those Thy children who are heirs of Thy glorious Kingdom; through. . .

For One's Children.

ALMIGHTY God, the Father and Maker of us all, Who of Thy blessing and goodness hast vouchsafed to make me a father of children: Be pleased also to accept my hearty thanksgiving and devout praise for the same; and grant me Thy heavenly grace and assistance so to train them up in Thy godly nurture, virtue, religion and discipline, that they may continually serve, honor, and obey Thee, their heavenly Father; and that Thou, acknowledging them and blessing them as Thy children here, mayst bring them to the blessing prepared for Thy children hereafter; through. . .

ALMIGHTY, Everlasting God, Merciful Father, since only the regenerate can see Thy kingdom and nothing is pleasing to Thee that hath not Thy Spirit: We beseech Thee that Thou wouldest grant to this child, who is Thy creation, Thy Holy Spirit of adoption, and seal and make sure his heart with the same, according to the promise of Thy dear Son, Jesus Christ; so that the inward renewal and regeneration of the Spirit through holy baptism may at all times be given him through Thy Divine working, and that he may be baptized into the death of Jesus Christ, be buried with Him and through Him be raised from the dead to walk in newness of life to the praise of the Glory of God and the good of his neighbor; through. . .

O LORD Jesus Christ, Who art the eternal wisdom of the Father: We beseech Thee to assist, with Thy heavenly grace, the good learning and godly discipline of our children, that in all and above all things they may attain the knowledge of Thee, Whom to know is life eternal; and that, according to the example of Thy holy childhood, as they grow in years they may grow in wisdom, and in favor with God and man; Who. . .

For a Friend.

O GOD, Who by the grace of the Holy Ghost hast poured the gifts of love into the hearts of Thy faithful people: Grant unto Thy servant(s), *N. N.,* for whom I implore Thy mercy, health of body and soul; that *he* (they) may love Thee with all *his* (their) strength, and with perfect affection fulfill Thy pleasure; through. . .

ALMIGHTY and everlasting God, have mercy upon Thy servant *N.,* and guide *him* according to Thy clemency into the way of everlasting salvation; that by Thy grace *he* may desire what pleases Thee, and with all power may perform it; through. . .

For Brethren and Friends in Distant Lands.

ALMIGHTY Father, Who art present in Thy power in every place: Give ear in Thy loving-kindness to the supplications which we offer unto Thee on behalf of our brethren and friends in distant lands; may Thy mighty hand shield and protect them from all evil; may Thy Holy Spirit guide them in the right way and bless their going out and their coming in; and grant that, being united by our fellowship with Thee, we may all at the last be gathered in the Home which is above; through. . .

For a Friend on his Birthday.

O GOD, the Life of the faithful, the Saviour and Guardian of those that fear Thee, Who, after the expiration of a year, hast been pleased to bring Thy servant *N.* to this *his* natural birthday: Increase in *him* the grace of the Protector of life, and multiply *his* days with many years, that having, by Thy favor, been carried through a happy life, *he* may be enabled to attain the height of heavenly joys; through. . .

FOR THE SICK

General.

SOVEREIGN Lord, our God Almighty, we beseech Thee to save us all, Thou only Physician of souls and bodies. Sanctify us all, Thou that healest every disease; and heal also *me* (*this*) Thy servant. Raise *me* (*him*) up from the bed of pain by Thy tender mercy, visit *me* (*him*) in mercy and compassion, drive away from *me* (*him*) all sickness and infirmity; that being raised up by Thy mighty hand, *I* (*he*) may serve Thee with all thankfulness; and that we, being made partakers of Thine ineffable benignity, may praise and glorify Thee, Who doest works great and wonderful, and worthy to be praised. For it is Thine to pity and to save; and to Thee we ascribe glory, Father, Son and Holy Ghost, now and forever, and unto ages of ages.

O GOD, Who ever governest Thy creatures with tender affection: Incline Thine ear to our supplications, and graciously regard Thy servant, who is suffering from bodily sickness; and visit *him* with Thy salvation, and bestow the medicine of heavenly grace; through. . .

O GOD, Who hast vouchsafed to mankind the remedies that bring salvation and the gifts of eternal life: Preserve to Thy servant the gifts of Thy power, and grant that not only in *his* body, but also in *his* soul, *he* may experience Thy healing; through. . .

Before Holy Communion for the Sick.

A LMIGHTY God, heavenly Father, since I can be well pleasing unto Thee only in Thy dear Son, my Lord Jesus Christ: So sanctify my body and soul, and grant that I receive His blessed communion in this Holy Supper with truly believing desire and thanksgiving, so that comforted again by Thy eternal blessings and love toward me, and strengthened in my faith, I may patiently suffer according to Thy will, obediently live, and when Thou wilt, blessedly die; through the Same. . .

A LMIGHTY, everlasting God, Creator of all things, according to Whose wisdom and power all things are controlled: Life and death are in Thy hand, and it hath been especially pleasing unto Thee to order the length of each man's life, gathering all his months

and days in a determined number, counting all
his steps beyond which he cannot walk: We
humbly beseech Thy godly mercy, if this
Thy servant has not yet completed the span
of *his* life, to restore to *him* the lost strength
to *his* body, and to raise *him* up again joyful
and well, from this bed of sickness, just as
Thy beloved Son, Jesus Christ, raised up
Peter's wife's mother, and restored the long
afflicted cripple at the pool's side to health,
commanding him to take up his bed and go to
his home, as a sign of the genuine health im-
parted him with his bodily cure: Grant, we
humbly beseech Thee, that this Thy servant
may in like manner experience the tenderness
of Thy love and the benediction of Thy healing, saving word, so that, with restored
powers, *he* may laud and praise Thy holy
name in Thy Church, and fashion the re-
mainder of *his* life after Thy holy will, and
with the increase of true, Christian faith be
the better prepared for *his* last hours and refreshed to serve Thee daily in constancy and
love; through Jesus Christ, our Lord. Amen.

ALMIGHTY God, merciful Father, Who
through Thy dear Son, Jesus Christ, hast
said unto us unworthy sinners: "Where two
or three are gathered together in His name,
and where they have agreed as touching a

matter to be sought of Thee out of Thy
bounty, there He will be in the midst and it
shall be done unto them according to their
faith": With this blessed comfort and assurance, we humbly come before Thee, bringing to Thee, much as did the four who carried the poor paralytic to Thy Son Christ,
this our *brother, N. N.*, whom Thou hast
touched with Thy hand; and beseech Thee
to behold our earnest prayer and humble
hearty confidence, granting us through the
inspiration of Thy Holy Spirit, to pray what
is right, and through Thy mercy, to strengthen
our faith in that Thou grantest gracious help
to this Thy sick servant, in order that *he* may
be restored to health or, be it Thy will, fall
asleep in Thee; through. . .

HEAR me, Almighty and most merciful God
and Saviour; extend Thine accustomed
goodness to me Thy humble servant who am
now grieved with sickness; visit me, O Lord,
as Thou didst visit Peter's wife's mother and
the centurion's servant; so visit and restore
unto me my former health (if it be Thy
blessed will) : or else give me grace so to take
Thy visitation, that, after this painful life is
ended, I may dwell with Thee in life everlasting; through. . .

O SWEET JESUS, I desire neither life nor death, but Thy most holy will; Thou art the thing, O Lord, that I look for; be it unto me according to Thy good pleasure. If it be Thy will to have me die, receive my soul; and grant that in Thee, and with Thee, I may receive everlasting rest. If it be Thy will to have me live any longer upon earth, give me grace to amend the rest of my life, and with good works to glorify Thy holy name; Who...

Thanksgiving for Recovery from Sickness.

O GOD, in Whose hand are the issues of life and death, Who of Thy great mercy didst raise up Thy servant Hezekiah, when sick unto death: We thank Thee that Thou hast restored this our *brother* from the gates of death, and we beseech Thee, that *he* may dedicate the life Thou hast preserved to Thy service, and finally be found worthy to enter the happy abode where sickness and death may never come; through. . .

FOR THOSE FOR WHOM I SHOULD PRAY

For the Laborer.

ALMIGHTY God, Who, when Thou didst send forth man from Eden, commandedst him to labor in the sweat of his brow: We acknowledge that all our toil and work is in vain if it be without Thy blessing and aid; and we humbly beseech Thee to assist us patiently to fulfill our calling, and faithfully to accomplish our work, graciously enriching it with Thy blessing, in order that the labor of our hands may prosper, and, in thankfulness, we may consecrate the fruits thereof to the spread of Thy Kingdom and the help of the needy; through. . .

For the Contrite.

O GOD, Who hast pity upon all, and ceasest not to receive with fatherly kindness them who return unto Thee: Remember, we beseech Thee, that we are but flesh, and be ready to turn Thy wrath away, nor kindle all that wrath against us, but soften it and vouchsafe us Thine, unfailing grace; through. . .

For the Outcasts.

O GOD, Who tellest the number of' the stars, and callest them all by their names: Heal, we beseech Thee, the contrite in heart, and gather together the outcasts, and enrich us with the fullness of Thy wisdom; through. . .

For the Distressed.

A LMIGHTY and Everlasting God, the Comfort of the sad, the Strength of sufferers, let the prayers of those that cry out of any tribulation come unto Thee; that all may rejoice to find that Thy mercy is present with them in their afflictions; through. . .

For the Afflicted.

U NTO every Christian soul that is afflicted, or plunged into distress, grant Thou mercy, grant relief, grant refreshment; through. . .

W E beseech Thee, O Lord, give strength to the weary, aid to the sufferers, comfort to the sad, help to those in tribulation; through. . .

For the Lapsed.

O LORD GOD of Israel, we beseech Thee, we entreat Thee, that Thou wouldst not refuse us sinners, because of our conversation. Thy goodness which Thou bestowest freely on them that are true of heart, that Thou mayest make them who are their own slaves rebel by that same grace whereby Thou rulest the lowly; and that the same goodness wherewith Thou ever crownest the righteous may continually interpose for us; that Thou mayest spare us sinners, that, rejoicing in the goodness wherein the saints are glad, they may delight in being restored by it to Thee, whom worldly lures have drawn from Thee through the contagion of divers things, and that with humble devotion of soul they may pay their vows unto Thee, uniting in Thy praise; through. . .

For the Iniquitous.

O GOD, Who hatest all that work iniquity: Fill us with the strength of Thy love; that they may at some time turn to Thee, and bitterly lament their sin, who now speak falsely against Thee; through. . .

For Unbelievers.

HEAR, Thou who rulest Joseph like a flock, stir up Thy strength and save them for whom Thou camest to be born on earth; Thou, Who hast vouchsafed to gain the multitude of the Gentiles by stretching forth to them the worship of faith: Deliver by the swift act of Thy loving kindness the souls of unbelievers from the pit of false doctrine, and bring them to Thyself to please Thee and trust in Thee; Who livest. . .

For Profaners of the Lord's Day.

O GOD, grant that they who, neglecting Thy worship on Thy holy day, give themselves rather to the business or pleasure of the world, may turn to Thee whilst it is yet time, and rise out of all carnal affections by the power of grace; so that they perish not in everlasting death when the world and its lusts shall have passed away, but, being found in Him Who died for us and rose again, may be saved by grace; through the Same. . .

For those who have none to pray for them.

O LORD JESUS CHRIST, Who ever lovest to make intercession for us: Let Thy mercy be extended to all those who have none upon earth to pray for them in Thy name, and bring them, for Thy sake, to a participation of Thy grace on earth, that they may praise Thee with all Thy saints in Thine everlasting glory. Amen.

In Old Age.

O GOD, unspeakable Mercy, go not far from us, make haste to help us, and forsake us not in our old age when we are grey headed; quicken us and comfort us in Thy love, and grant that we may ever worthily sing the majesty of Thy glory; through. . .

For the Dying.

UNTO Thee, O Lord, we commend the soul of Thy servant, *N.*, that dying to the world, *he* may live to Thee, and whatever sins *he* has committed through the frailty of earthly life, do Thou clear away by Thy most loving and merciful forgiveness; through. . .

LORD Jesus Christ, Redeemer and Restorer of mankind, we beseech Thee graciously to open the gate of paradise to Thy servants returning to Thee from this present world, that, being delivered from the suffering and

sin of this world, they may depart rejoicing
to that heavenly country, where death and
sorrow are no more, but sweetest joy and end-
less gladness abide for evermore; Who
livest. . .

For a Happy Death.

O GOD, Who art the Saviour of all the
living, Who willest not the death of
sinners, nor rejoicest in the perdition of those
that die, I humbly entreat Thee to vouchsafe
me pardon of my offences, that I may bewail
what I have committed, and henceforth commit them no more; and that when my last day
and the end of my life has arrived, Thy holy
angels may receive me cleansed from all offences; through. . .

For Those in Sorrow.

O HEAVENLY Father, Whose blessed
Son Jesus Christ did weep at the grave
of Lazarus His friend: Look, we beseech
Thee, with compassion upon those who are
now in sorrow and affliction: comfort them,
O Lord, with Thy gracious consolations;
make them to know that all things work together for good to them that love Thee; and
grant them evermore sure trust and con-

fidence in Thy fatherly care; through the
Same. . .

In Commemoration of the Faithful Departed.

ALMIGHTY GOD, with Whom do live the
spirits of them that depart hence in the
Lord, and with Whom the souls of the faithful, after they are delivered from the burden
of the flesh, are in joy and felicity: We praise
and magnify Thy Holy Name for all Thy servants who have finished their course in Thy
faith and fear; and we most humbly beseech
Thee that, at the day of the general resurrection, we, and all they who are of the mystical
body of Thy Son, may be set on his right
hand, and hear that His most joyful voice,
"Come ye blessed of My Father, inherit the
kingdom prepared for you from the foundation of the world." Grant this, O most merciful Father, for the sake of Jesus Christ, our
only Mediator and Advocate; Who. .

ALMIGHTY GOD, the God of the spirits of all flesh, Who by a voice from
Heaven didst proclaim, "Blessed are the dead
who die in the Lord": Multiply, we beseech
Thee, to those who rest in Jesus, the manifold
blessings of Thy love, that the good work
which Thou didst begin in them may be per-

fected unto the day of Jesus Christ; and of Thy mercy, O Heavenly Father, vouchsafe that we, who now serve Thee here on earth, may at the last, together with them, be found meet to be partakers of the inheritance of the saints in light; for the sake of the Same. . .

GENERAL PRAYERS

ALMIGHTY and Merciful God, the Fountain of all goodness, Who knowest the thoughts of our hearts, we confess unto Thee that we have sinned against Thee, and done evil in Thy sight; wash us, we beseech Thee, from the stains of our past sins, and give us grace and power to put away all hurtful things; so that, being delivered from the bondage of sin, we may bring forth worthy fruits of repentance. O eternal Light, shine into our hearts. O eternal Goodness, deliver us from evil. O eternal Power, be Thou our support. Eternal Wisdom, scatter the darkness of our ignorance. Eternal Pity, have mercy upon us. Grant unto us that with all our hearts and minds and strength we may evermore seek Thy face; and finally bring us, in Thine infinite mercy, to Thy holy presence; through. . .

O GOD, Thou art Life, Wisdom, Truth, Bounty and Blessedness, the eternal and only true God! My God and my Lord, Thou art my Hope and my heart's Joy. I confess, with thanksgiving, that Thou hast made me in Thine image, that I may direct all my thoughts to Thee and love Thee. Lord, make me to know Thee aright, that I may more and more love and enjoy and possess Thee. And since in the life here below, I cannot fully attain this blessedness, let it at least grow in me day by day, until it all be fulfilled at last in the life to come. Here be the knowledge of Thee increased, and there let it be perfected. Here let my love to Thee grow, and there let it ripen, that my joy being here great in hope, may there in fruition be made perfect; through. . .

LORD, without Thee I can do nothing; with Thee I can do all. Help me by Thy grace, that I fall not; help me by Thy strength, to resist mightily the very first beginnings of evil, before it takes hold of me; help me to cast myself at once at Thy sacred feet, and lie still there, until the storm be overpast; and, if I lose sight of Thee, bring me back quickly to Thee, and grant me to love Thee better, for Thy tender mercy's sake in Jesus Christ, my Lord.

O GOD, the Father of our Saviour, JESUS CHRIST, Whose name is great, Whose nature is blissful, Whose goodness is inexhaustible, God and Ruler of all things, Who art blessed forever, before Whom stand thousands, ten thousand times ten thousand, the hosts of holy angels and archangels: Sanctify, O Lord, my soul and body and spirit, search my conscience, and cast out of me every evil thought, every base desire, all envy and pride, all wrath and anger, and all that is contrary to Thy holy will; and grant me, O Lord, lover of men, with a pure heart and a contrite soul, to call upon Thee, our holy God and Father Who art in heaven; through. . .

LORD, I know not what I ought to ask of Thee, Thou only knowest what I need, Thou lovest me better than I know how to love myself. O Father, give to Thy child that which he himself knows not how to ask. I dare not ask either for crosses or consolations; I simply present myself before Thee, I open my heart to Thee. Behold my needs which I know not myself; see and do according to Thy tender mercy. Smite, or heal; depress me, or raise me up; I adore all Thy purposes without knowing them; I am silent, I offer myself in sacrifice; I yield myself to Thee; I would have no other desire than to accomplish Thy will. Teach me to pray;—pray Thyself in me. . . through Jesus Christ, my Lord.

O ALMIGHTY GOD, give to Thy servant a meek and gentle spirit, that I may be slow to anger, and easy to mercy and forgiveness. Give me a wise and constant heart, that I may never be moved to an intemperate anger for any injury that is done or offered. Lord, let me ever be courteous, and easy to be entreated; let me never fall into a peevish or contentious spirit, but follow peace with all men; offering forgiveness, inviting them by courtesies, ready to confess my own errors, apt to make amends, and desirous to be reconciled. Let no sickness, cross or accident, no employment or weariness, make me angry or ungentle and discontented, or unthankful, but in all things make me like unto the Holy Jesus, through Whom I humbly come to Thee. . . REV. THEO. DELANEY

O THOU gracious, gentle and loving God, Thou God of peace, Father of mercy, God of all comfort; see, I lament before Thee the evil of my heart; I acknowledge that I am too much disposed to anger, jealousy and revenge, to ambition and pride, which often give rise to discord and bitter feeling between me and others. Too often have I thus offended and grieved both Thee, O long-suffering Father, and my fellow-men. O forgive me this sin, and suffer me to partake of the blessing which Thou hast promised to the peace-makers, who shall be called Thy children. Bestow on me, O Lord, a genial spirit and unwearied forbearance; a mild, loving and patient heart; kindly looks, pleasant, cordial speech and manners in the intercourse of daily life; that I may give offence to none, but as much as in me lies live in love with all men; through. . .

I OFFER up unto Thee my prayers and intercessions for those especially who have in any manner hurt, grieved, or found fault with me, or who have done me any damage or displeasure. . . For all those also whom at any time I have vexed, troubled, burdened, and scandalized, by words or deeds, knowingly or in ignorance; that Thou wouldst grant us all equally pardon for our sins, and for our offences against each other. . . Take away from our hearts, O Lord, all suspiciousness, indignation, wrath, and contention, and whatsoever may hurt charity and lessen brotherly love. Have mercy, O Lord, have mercy on those that crave Thy mercy; through. . .

AH LORD, unto Whom all hearts are open, Thou canst govern the vessel of my soul far better than I can. Arise, O Lord, and command the stormy wind and the troubled sea of my heart to be still, and be at peace in Thee, that I may look up to Thee undisturbed, and abide in union with Thee, my Lord. Let me not be carried hither and thither by wandering thoughts; but forgetting all else, let me see and hear Thee. Renew my spirit; kindle in me Thy light; that it may shine within me, and my heart may burn in love and adoration towards Thee. Let Thy Holy Spirit dwell in me continually, and make me Thy temple and sanctuary, and fill me with divine love and light and life, with devout and heavenly thoughts, with comfort and strength, with joy and peace; through. . .

O GOD, my everlasting Refuge, with grateful heart, I lay at Thy feet the folded hours when Thou knowest me, but I know Thee not; and with joy receive from Thy hand once more my open task and conscious communion with Thy life and thought. Day by day liken me more to the spirits of the departed wise and good; and fit me in my generation to carry on their work till I am ready for more perfect union with them above. And if ever I faint under any appointed cross and say, "It is too hard to bear," may I look to the steps of the Man of Sorrows toiling on to Calvary, and pass freely into Thy hand, and become one with Him and

Thee. Dedicate me to the joyful service of Thy will; and own me as Thy child in time and eternity; through. . .

GIVE me, O Lord, purity of lips, a clean and innocent heart, and rectitude of action. Give me humility, patience, abstinence, chastity, prudence, justice, fortitude, temperance. Give me the Spirit of wisdom and understanding, the Spirit of counsel and strength, the Spirit of knowledge and godliness, and of Thy fear. Make me ever to seek Thy face with all my heart, all my soul, all my mind; grant me to have a contrite and humble heart in Thy presence, to prefer nothing to Thy love. Most high, eternal and ineffable Wisdom, drive away from me the darkness of blindness and ignorance; most high and eternal Strength, deliver me; most high and eternal Fortitude, assist me; most high and incomprehensible Light, illuminate me; most high and infinite Mercy, have mercy on me; through. . .

O GOD, to Whom all the earth sings loud praise in rejoicing, and Whose glory it proclaims with the tuneful voice of a psalm, Whose awful might in Thy works it confesses: Grant that our voices may yield Thee acceptable praise, and our prayers give Thee a perfect psalm, and celebrate Thee, the Maker of all powers; and inasmuch as Thine eyes behold the nations, and invisibly search the inmost parts of all things: we beseech Thee so to look on us graciously with Thine eyes, and to correct us so in mercy, that Thou mayest not pour Thy wrath upon us, angered by our misdeeds, nor restrain Thy mercy when Thou art entreated; and grant that our very fear of Thee for our sins may be our chastisement, and our belief and confession of Thy Godhead the reward of our pardon. Set our souls then, O Lord, unto life, that we may weep here for our doings, and rejoice there in Thy mercy; through. . .

MORNING PRAYERS

Lord's Day Morning.

MOST glorious Trinity, in Thy mercy, I commit to Thee, this day, my soul, my body, all my ways and goings, all my deeds and purposes. I pray Thee so to open my heart and mouth, that I may praise Thy Name, Which of all names alone is holy; and since Thou hast created me for the praise of Thy holy name, grant that my life may be to Thine honor, and that I may serve Thee in Thy love and fear. Amen.

O GOD, Who givest us not only the day for labor, and the night for rest, but also the peace of this blessed day: We beseech Thee that this season of holy quiet may be profitable to us in heavenly things, and refresh and strengthen us to finish the work which Thou hast given us to do; through. . .

FROM the night my spirit awaketh unto Thee, O God, for Thy precepts are a light unto me. Teach me, O God, Thy righteousness, Thy commandments and Thy judgments.

Enlighten the eyes of my mind that I sleep not into the death of sin. Drive away all darkness from my heart. Vouchsafe to me the Sun of Righteousness. Guard my life from all reproach by the seal of Thy Holy Spirit. Guide my steps into the way of peace. Through. . .

GRANT us, O Lord, to pass this day in gladness and peace, without stumbling and without stain, that reaching the eventide victorious over all temptation, we may praise Thee, the eternal God, Who art blessed, and dost govern all things throughout the ages. Through Thy mercy. . .

General.

O GOD, Who in the daytime commandest Thy mercy, and in the night season manifestest Thyself: We pray Thee that Thou wouldest both in the day defend us for our salvation, and in the night protect us for our rest; through. . .

O MERCIFUL Lord God, Heavenly Father, I render most high laud, praise and thanks unto Thee, that Thou hast preserved me both this night. and all the times and days of my life hitherto, under Thy protection, and

hast suffered me to live until this present hour;
and I beseech Thee heartily, that Thou wilt
vouchsafe to receive me this day, and the
residue of my whole life, from henceforth into
Thy good keeping, ruling and governing me
with Thy Holy Spirit, that all manner of darkness and evil may be utterly chased and driven
out of my heart; and that I may walk in the
light of Thy truth, to Thy glory and praise,
and to the help and furtherance of my neighbor; through. . .

ALMIGHTY God, Who hast planted the
Day-Star in the Heavens, and scattering
the night, dost restore morning to the world:
Fill us, we beseech Thee, with Thy mercy, so
that Thou being our Enlightener, all the darkness of our sins may be dispersed; through. . .

PRAISED be Thou, O God, almighty Ruler,
Who dost make the day bright with Thy
sunshine, and the night with the beams of
heavenly fire; harken to our prayers, and
forgive us both our conscious and unconscious
transgressions; clothe us with Thy truth;
watch over us with Thy power; save us from
all calamity; and give us grace to pass all the
days of our life, blameless, holy, peaceful,
free from sin, terror and offence; for with
Thee is mercy and plenteous redemption, our

Lord and God, and to Thee we bring our
thanks and praise; through. . .

WE give Thee thanks, O Lord our God,
for all Thy goodness at all times and in
all places, because Thou hast shielded, rescued,
helped and guided us all the days of our
lives, and brought us unto this hour. We
pray and beseech Thee, merciful God, to grant
in Thy goodness, that we may spend this day,
and all the time of our lives, without sin, in
fullness of joy, holiness and reverence of
Thee; but drive away from us, O Lord, all
envy, fear and temptations. Bestow upon us
what is good and meet. Whatever sin we
commit in thought, word, or deed, do Thou
in Thy goodness and mercy, pardon. And
lead us not into temptation, but deliver us
from evil, through the grace, mercy and love
of Thy Only-Begotten Son. . .

O LORD God, King of heaven and earth,
may it please Thee this day to order and
hallow, to rule and govern our hearts and
bodies, our thoughts, words and works, according to Thy commandments, that we, being
helped by Thee, may here and forever and
ever, be delivered and saved through. . .

O LORD our God, Who hast chased the slumber from our eyes, and once more assembled us to lift up our hands unto Thee, and to praise Thy just judgments: Accept our prayers and supplications, and give us faith that maketh not ashamed, confident hope and love unfeigned; bless our coming in and going out, our thoughts, words, and works, and let us begin this day with the praise of the unspeakable sweetness of Thy mercy. Hallowed be Thy name; Thy kingdom come; through. . .

INTO the hands of Thy blessed protection, and unspeakable mercy, O Lord, I commend this day my soul and body, with all the faculties, powers and actions of them both, beseeching Thee to be ever with me, to direct, sanctify and govern me in the ways of Thy laws, and in the works of Thy commandments; that through Thy most mighty protection, both here and ever, I may be preserved in body and soul, to serve Thee, the only true God; through. . .

Morning Prayers from the Gelasianum.

WE give Thee thanks, holy Lord, Father Almighty, everlasting God, Who hast been pleased to bring us through the night to the hours of morning, we pray Thee to grant us to pass this day without sin, so that at eventide we may again give thanks to Thee; through. . .

RISING from our beds, we implore, O Lord, in our morning prayers, the assistance of Thy grace, so that, the darkness of our vices being dispersed, we may be enabled to walk in the light of virtues; through. . .

O LORD, mercifully regard the hearty desires of Thy humble servants which are breathed unto Thee in the morning, and enlighten the secrets of our hearts with the eyesalve of Thy fatherly goodness, so that dark desires may no longer enslave those whom the light of heavenly grace hath restored; through. . .

O LORD, we humbly beseech Thee, the true Light and Author of light, that Thou wouldst vouchsafe to drive away from us the darkness of our vices, and to illuminate us with the light of virtues; through. . .

INCREASE in us, O Lord, we beseech Thee, faith in Thee, and kindle within us the light of Thy Holy Spirit evermore; through. . .

O GOD, Who dividest the day from the night: Separate our actions from the gloom of darkness, that we, ever meditating things which are holy, may live perpetually in Thy praise; through. . .

SEND forth, we beseech Thee, O Lord, Thy light into our hearts, and grant that we, walking by the constant light of Thy commandments, and in Thy way, may not in anything be beguiled by error; through. . .

LET Thy truth, we beseech Thee, O Lord, shine in our hearts, and let every wile of the enemy be brought to nought; through. . .

WE give unspeakable thanks to Thy goodness, O Almighty God, Who, having chased away the gloom of night, hast brought us to the beginning of this day, and also, having removed the blindness of our ignorance, hast recalled us to the worship and knowledge of Thy name. Illuminate our understandings, Almighty Father, that we, walking in the light of Thy precepts, may follow Thee as our Guide and King; through. . .

GOD, Who dispellest the darkness of ignorance by the light of Thy Word: Increase in our hearts that grace of faith, which Thou Thyself hast given us; so that the fire

which Thy grace hath caused to be kindled,
may not be extinguished by any temptations;
through. . .

GRACIOUSLY pour into our understand-
ings, O Lord, Thy holy light, that we
may be evermore devoted unto Thee, by
Whose wisdom we were created and by
Whose providence we are governed; through
Jesus Christ, our Lord.

EVENING PRAYERS

Lord's Day Evening.

HAIL, gladd'ning Light, of His pure glory
      poured,
   Who is the Immortal Father,
Heavenly, blest,
Holiest of holies,
JESUS CHRIST, our Lord!
   Now we are come to the sun's hour of
     rest,
  The lights of ev'ning round us shine,
   We hymn
  The Father, Son and Holy Ghost Divine.
Worthiest art Thou at all times to be sung
       Son of our God,
     Giver of Life, alone;
    Therefore in all the world,
     Thy glories, Lord,
      They own.
        Amen.

IN the evening, and morning, and noon-
  day, we praise Thee, we bless Thee, we
thank Thee, and pray Thee, Master of all, to
direct our prayer as incense before Thee; and
let not our hearts turn away to words or

thoughts of wickedness; but rescue us from all things that hurt our souls. For to Thee, Lord, Lord, our eyes look up, and our hope is in Thee. Confound us not, O our God; through. . .

O LORD God, the Life of mortals, the Light of the faithful, the Strength of those who labor, and the Repose of the dead: Grant us a quiet night free from all disturbance; that after an interval of quiet sleep, we may, by Thy bounty, at the return of light, be endued with activity from the Holy Spirit, and enabled in peace to render thanks to Thee; through. . .

WATCH over us, O Lord, heavenly Father, and preserve us from every evil which may happen to the body and soul. Grant us grace to take our rest this night in safety beneath Thy protection. Guard and bless Thy Church and this Thy congregation. Graciously remember, in Thy mercy, those who are in sickness, in need, and in peril. Have mercy upon all mankind; and when at length our last evening cometh grant us then to fall asleep in Thy peace, that we may awake in Thy glory; through. . .

General.

O LORD, Who hast delivered us from every arrow that flieth by day, deliver us also from everything that walketh in darkness; vouchsafe also that we may pass the course of this night without sin or temptation of evil, and deliver us from all terror and dread which cometh to us from the evil one; through. . .

O LORD, our heavenly Father, Almighty and Everlasting God, by Whose providence both the day and night are governed: Vouchsafe, we beseech Thee, as Thou hast this day preserved us by Thy goodness, so still this night to shadow us under the blessed wing of Thy mighty protection, and to cover us with Thy heavenly mercy, that neither the princes of darkness may have any power over us, nor the works of darkness overwhelm us; but that we, being armed with Thy defence, may be preserved from all adversities that may hurt the body, and from all wicked thoughts which may assault and defile the soul; through. . .

ABIDE with us, O good Lord, through the night, guarding, keeping, guiding, sustaining, sanctifying, and with Thy love gladdening us, that in Thee we may ever live, and in Thee we may die; through. . .

VISIT, we beseech Thee, O Lord, this habitation, and drive from it all snares of the enemy: Let Thy holy angels dwell herein to keep us in peace, and may Thy blessing always be upon us; through. . .

O BLESSED GOD, Who neither slumberest nor sleepest, take us into Thy gracious keeping for this night, and make us mindful of that night where the noise of this busy world shall be heard by us no more. O Lord, in Whom we trust, help us by Thy grace so to live, that we may never be afraid to die, and grant that at the last, as now, our vesper hymn may be: I will lay me down in peace and sleep, for Thou, Lord, makest me dwell in safety; through. . .

O LORD, our God, refresh us with quiet sleep when we are wearied with the day's work, that being assisted with the help which our weakness needs, we may be devoted to Thee both in body and soul: through . . .

BE PRESENT, O merciful God, and protect us through the silent hours of this night so that we who are fatigued by the changes and chances of this fleeting world, may repose upon Thine eternal changelessness; through. . .

For Saturday Evening.

O ALMIGHTY GOD, Who after the creation of the world, didst rest from all Thy works, and, as an image of Thine own, didst sanctify a day of rest for Thy creatures: Grant to us that, putting away all earthly cares and anxieties, we may be duly prepared for the services of Thy sanctuary; and that our rest here on earth may be a preparation for the eternal Sabbath promised to Thine elect in heaven; through. . .

Before Going to Rest.

AH SWEET JESUS, pierce the marrow of my soul with the healing shafts of Thy love, that it may truly burn, and melt, and languish, with the only desire of Thee; that it may desire to be dissolved and to be with Thee; let it hunger only for the Bread of Life; let it thirst after Thee, the Spring and Fountain of eternal light, the Stream of true pleasure; let it always desire Thee, seek Thee, and find Thee, and sweetly rest in Thee; Who livest. . .

Pillow-Prayers.

I COMMEND myself, and mine, and all who are dear to me, to Him Who is able to keep us from falling, and to present us faultless before the presence of His glory, to the only wise God and our Saviour, to Whom be glory and majesty, dominion and power, now and forever. Amen.

GOD, the Father, bless me;
    God, the Son, defend me;
God, the Holy Ghost, preserve me,
Now and forever. Amen.

IN PREPARATION FOR PARISH WORK

General.

ENLARGE our souls with a divine charity, O blessed God, that we may hope all things, endure all things, and become messengers of Thy healing mercy to the grievances and infirmities of men; in all things attune our hearts to the holiness and harmony of Thy kingdom; and hasten the time when Thy kingdom shall come, and Thy will be done on earth as it is in heaven; through. . .

TEACH me, Good Lord, to serve Thee as Thou deservest to be served; to give and not to count the cost; to fight and not to heed the wounds; to toil and not to seek for rest; to labor and not to ask for any reward save that of knowing that I am doing Thy will. Amen.

O GOD of all goodness and all grace, Who art worthy of a greater love than I can either give or understand: Fill my heart with such love toward Thee that nothing may seem too hard for me to do or to suffer in obedience

to Thy will; and grant that thus loving Thee,
I may become more like unto Thee daily, and
finally obtain the crown of life which Thou
hast promised to those who love Thee;
through. . .

O BLESSED JESUS, Who didst bid all
those who carry heavy burdens to come
unto Thee: Refresh us with Thy presence, and
Thy power; and crown Thy choice of us to
be Thy ministers by making us springs of
strength and joy for those whom Thou hast
sent us to serve; Who livest. . .

For Charity.

O GOD, Who by Thy holy apostle hast
taught us to be all things to all men for
the salvation of souls: Mercifully grant that
endued with the Spirit of Thy love, I may
win souls unto Thee, and attain eternal life;
through. . .

For Humility.

O GOD, Who raisest up in the hearts of
faithful pastors the Spirit of Thy Son
to preach the gospel to the poor, and to relieve
the distresses of the sick and sorrowful:
Grant unto me, I beseech Thee, a full portion

of the same Spirit, that in humility and love I may so minister unto the necessities of those committed to my charge, as with them to be a partaker of everlasting consolation; through. . .

For Consecration.

LORD God the Holy Ghost, Promise of the Father, Comforter and Sanctifier: Take of the things of Christ and fill us, that having found all in Him, been built up in faith and filled with His love, we may be enabled by Thy perpetual Light warming our cold hearts to give over our whole selves to unselfish service, and find in whatever task or burden the gladsome blessing of consecration to Father, Son and Thee; and in every victory over temptation, wrong and sin, the peace of God which passeth understanding; Who livest and reignest with the Father and the Son, One God, world without end. Amen.

TAKE our wills, conform them unto Thine, O Lord Jesus; take our hearts, fill them with Thy love; take our lips, speak through them to Thy kingdom's spread; take our lives, use them them to Thy blessed purpose; take us, Lord, body, soul and spirit, make us vessels of Thy grace, examples of Thy teaching; take us

Lord, that we take not ourselves from Thee;
and in the end, take us to Thyself, where
Thou, O blessed Jesus, livest and reignest. . .

For Moral Courage.

GRANT us, O Lord, such boldness in Thee
that we may set our faces as a flint, and
not be ashamed, but, contending valiantly for
the Truth, may out of weakness be made
strong, and conquer in Thy might; through...

For Earnestness.

GRANT us, O Lord, spotless purity of life,
and ardent zeal for the salvation of souls,
that in all good works and steadfast faith we
may preach Thee, and through Thy mercy, at
length come unto Thee, Who art the Author
and Giver of everlasting blessedness; through
. . .

For Perseverance.

O GOD, Who bestowest this upon us by
Thy grace, that we should be made
righteous instead of ungodly, blessed instead
of miserable: Be present to Thine own works,
be present to Thine own gifts; that they in
whom dwells a justifying faith may not lack
a strong perseverance; through. . .

BLESS me, O God, with the vision of Thy being and beauty, that in the strength of it, we may work without haste and without rest; through. . .

For Joy.

WHO can be worthy of this office unless he be first fitted for it by Thy preventing grace and compassion? Since, then, it is of Thy gift, not of our merit, Thou must also interpose Thy guidance, that it may not prove the everlasting punishment of our negligence, but rather be our constant joy. Grant this, Lord, through. . .

For Ministerial Success.

O GOD, Who employest men to plant and water Thy vineyard, whilst Thou alone givest the increase: Grant Thy grace unto Thy fellow-workers, endue them with power to convince the world of sin, and to set forth righteousness. Give them grace to wait on their preaching with earnest prayer, devout study, humble painstaking; strengthen them to plant and water, and do Thou, O Lord, give the increase; through. . .

For One's Parishioners.

O ETERNAL, merciful God, heavenly Father, I beseech Thee for all who are committed to my cure of souls and to my prayer. Grant them all grace and Thy Holy Spirit, that they may confess Thee and Thy dear Son Jesus Christ; grow in right faith, fear and love; and, in unswerving hope, in a Christian, repentant life, abide in Thy will and obedience faithfully to their end. Grant also to me, dear Father, grace to walk before them with a good life and to impart to them pure instruction, and grant that we all, guarded against impure faith and evil life, may come to everlasting salvation : through...

For the Children of the Parish.

MASTER and Saviour, Who hast told us that we must be as the little children in order to come to Thy kingdom, and Who didst love and bless them most tenderly: Grant that our children may be drawn to Thee by Thy Good Spirit and ever kept in Thy service, so that walking in Thy way, they may ever show forth Thy praise and be one with us in the confession of Thy holy name; Who livest. . .

O LORD Jesus, Lover of men, Who didst take little children in Thy arms and bless them: Grant me so to love and tenderly protect the little ones committed to my care, that I may by word and example bring them to Thee and teach them to know and love Thee, and trust in Thy protection; Who livest. . .

For the Catechumens.

ALMIGHTY God, heavenly Father, since our salvation depends upon a right knowledge of Thy holy Word, we beseech Thee therefore, to grant to these children, who have gathered in Thy name, that, their hearts being freed of all worldly thoughts and attractions, they may, with all diligence and earnestness, devoutly hear and grasp Thy holy Word, so that daily they may grow in the saving knowledge of Thy truth, believe in the holy gospel with all their hearts and persevere faithfully in obedience to Thy will to the end; through . . .

Before Bible School.

O HEAVENLY Father, Whose blessed Son hath said, "Suffer the little children to come unto Me": Prosper with Thy blessing the work of all who labor for the instruction and up-bringing of the young in virtue and true godliness, especially in our Bible school; grant that as the minds of Thy children are enlightened with knowledge, so their hearts may be daily drawn to the love of Thee and of Thy only Son, our Saviour; Who. . .

O ALMIGHTY God, Whose Only-Begotten Son out of great love for His Father's House abode three days in the Temple, being found there by His mother, seated in the midst of the teachers: We pray Thee, grant also to these children eagerness to abide in Thy house, to cling gladly to Thy Word and its, saving teaching; increase in them knowledge and wisdom and let them grow in all virtues and obedience to Thee and their fellowmen and thereby reach the fullness of the stature of manhood in Jesus Christ, Thy Son, our Lord; Who. . .

IN CONNECTION WITH DIVINE SERVICE

On Going to Church.

HOW amiable are Thy tabernacles, O Lord of Hosts.

LORD, open Thou my lips and purify my heart, that I may worthily magnify Thy glorious name; through. . .

On Entering the Church.

O LORD, open Thou my lips to praise Thy name, for I would adore Thee in Thy Church, O Blessed GOD, FATHER, SON, and HOLY SPIRIT, Who art worthy of all adoration and worship, blessing and praise, now and evermore. Amen.

I BELIEVE in Thee, O God, the Father, my Maker; I believe in Thee, O God, the Son, my Saviour; I believe in Thee, O God, the Holy Ghost, my Helper. Glory be to Thee O Holy Trinity. Amen.

FORGIVE, O God, for Jesus' sake, my many sins and faults, that joyfully I may worship Thee; grant me Thy Holy Spirit, to direct my thought, nourish me in Thy Word; and lead me to Thy altar, where in the communion of Thy Christ, I may be one in Him, and so live in Him to Thy praise; through the Same. . .

O GOD, Whose Word is a light making bright my way to Thee: Open my ears to hear, my mind to understand, my heart and soul to absorb, my life to show forth, Thy blessed word borne to me this day; through. . .

O GOD, Whom to know is to live. . .p. 21.

Before or After any Office.

O MERCIFUL GOD let that which is performed by our humble ministration, be fulfilled by Thy effectual power; through. . .

BE present, O merciful God, that what has been done by our office and ministry, may be confirmed by Thy blessing; through. . .

In the Sacristy.

THE GOD of our Lord Jesus Christ, and through Him, the Father of us all, grant that His godly name be hallowed, His kingdom increased, His divine will accomplished and that all that would hinder this be entirely done away, to the end, that we, in righteous Christian faith and with the fruits of good works, may live, glorify and praise Him, together with the Son and the Holy Ghost, the one, eternal, true God; for His is the kingdom, and the power, and the glory in eternity Amen.

GOD and Master of all things, make us the unworthy, O Lover of men, worthy of this hour, that we, remaining pure from all guile and all hypocrisy, may be united together by the bond of peace and love, being stablished by the sanctification of Thy divine knowledge, through Thy Only-Begotten Son, our Lord and Saviour Jesus Christ, with Whom. . .

LORD and Giver of Life, Supplier of good things, Thou Who didst give to men the blessed hope of everlasting life, our Lord Jesus Christ: Vouchsafe that we may in holiness accomplish this divine liturgy to Thee, to the enjoyment of future blessedness; to the end that we, ever guarded by Thy might and conducted to the light of truth, may send up to Thee glory and thanksgiving, Father, Son and Holy Ghost, now and ever.

WE beseech Thee, the Father of the Only-Begotten, the Lord of the universe, the Creator of the creatures, the Maker of things that have been made; clean hands do we stretch out, and our thoughts do we unfold to Thee. We pray Thee, have compassion, spare, benefit, improve, multiply us in virtue and faith and knowledge. Visit us, O Lord; to Thee we display our own weaknesses. Be propitious and have pity on us all in common. Have pity, benefit this people. Make it gentle and sober-minded and clean; and send angelic powers in order that all this Thy people may be holy and reverent. I beseech Thee, send the Holy Spirit into our mind and give us grace to learn the Divine Scriptures from Thy Spirit, and to interpret cleanly and worthily that all the flock present may be helped, through Thy Only-Begotten Jesus Christ in the Holy Spirit through Whom to Thee be the glory and the strength both now and unto all the ages of the ages. Amen.

LORD our God, great, eternal, wonderful, in glory, Who keepest covenant and promises for those that love Thee with their whole heart; Who art the life of all, the Help of those that flee unto Thee, the Hope of those who cry unto Thee: Cleanse me from my sin, secret and open, and from every thought displeasing to Thy goodness; cleanse my body and soul, my heart and conscience, that with a pure heart and a clean soul, with perfect love and calm hope, I may venture confidently and fearlessly, to minister before Thee, and pray unto Thee; through. . .

LORD JESUS, Thou great Arch-Shepherd, it is Thy office in which I serve; it is Thy work, which I do; it is Thy altar, to which I go; it is Thy Word, which I preach; it is Thy precious, redeemed congregation that I am to edify and build up on the foundation of our most holy faith; it is Thy glory, that I seek: Therefore, graciously assist me in this worship that I may minister and complete all according to Thy most holy will; Who livest . . .

O LORD, my gracious and faithful God, from Whom cometh all help and blessing: Send the Holy Spirit from Thy dwelling place and strengthen me for this service, that I, purified by Thee, may stand in this holy place and bring to Thee holy offerings; through. . .

O MY God, heavenly Father, Thou Lord of hosts, I thank Thee for this exceeding grace, that I dare to serve Thee, this day, at Thine altar; and that, prostrate at Thy feet, I may, for my sins and ignorance, and for the sins and ignorance of the people, supplicate Thy mercy: Hear, then, my humble prayer and keep me pure in Thy service; and grant me power of Thy Holy and Hallowing Spirit, that by His mediation, with a conscience free from sin, I may glorify Thee, and call upon Thee in all my ways, and that Thou mayest be gracious to me according to the fulness of Thy mercy; through. . .

CLEANSE me, O Lord, and purify my heart, that washed in the blood of the Lamb, I may attain everlasting joys; through the Same. . .

While Vesting.

GIVE me again, Lord, the robe of immortality, which I lost by the sin of the first parents, and although I am unworthy to come unto Thy holy sacrament, grant that I may attain everlasting joy; Who livest. . .

As Occasion Permits.

INCLINE Thine ears, O most merciful God, to our prayers, and illuminate our heart by the grace of the Holy Spirit, that I may worthily minister before Thee and love Thee with an eternal love; through. . .

O GOD, to Whom every heart is open, every desire known, from Whom no secret is hid: Purify the thoughts of our hearts by the inspiration of the Holy Spirit, that we may love Thee perfectly and praise Thee worthily; through. . .

LET the Paraclete, Who proceedeth from Thee, illuminate our minds, we beseech Thee, O Lord, and may He lead us into all truth, as Thy Son hath promised; through the Same. . .

GOD, Who didst teach the hearts of the faithful by the enlightenment of the Holy Spirit: Give to us, in the same Spirit, to think rightly, and through His consolation, to rejoice always; through. . .

VISIT and cleanse our consciences, Lord, we beseech Thee: That coming, our Lord, Jesus Christ, Thy Son, may find in us a mansion prepared for Himself; through the Same. . .

For Choirs.

O GOD in Whose temple at Jerusalem were appointed singers and those skilled in instruments of music to set forth Thy praises: Be present, we beseech Thee, with us Thy servants, and grant that in this our service we may worship Thee in spirit and in truth, and at last be found meet to glorify Thy name in Thy temple which is on high; through. . .

O GOD, to Whom the Cherubim and Seraphim adoringly sing, Holy, Holy, Holy: Grant that as our voices are uplifted in this service to Thy praise, so we may continually sing and make melody in our hearts unto Thee; through. . .

SHORT OFFICE BEFORE ENTERING THE SANCTUARY

✠

IN the Name of the Father. . .

The Psalm, *after which is to be said*: Glory be to the Father. . .

Psalms 84, 86, 130, 43.

Lord have mercy upon us.
Christ have mercy upon us.
Lord have mercy upon us.

Our Father, Who art in Heaven. . .

V. I said, O Lord, be merciful unto me.
R. Heal my soul, for I have sinned against Thee,

Turn Thee again, O Lord, at the last.
And be gracious unto Thy servants.

Let Thy priests be clothed with righteousness.
And let Thy saints shout for joy.

Cleanse me, O Lord, from secret faults.
And keep back Thy servant from pre-
sumptuous sins.

O Lord, hear my prayer.
And let my cry come unto Thee.

(*Collects as above.* p. 127ff.)

IN THE SANCTUARY

On Going to the Altar.

IN the Name of the Father, and of the Son, and of the Holy Ghost. Amen.

I will go unto the altar of God, even unto the God of my joy and gladness.

In the multitude of Thy mercies, O Lord, I go unto Thine altar. O save and deliver me for Thy mercies' sake. Amen.

Before the Altar.

GLORY be to Thee, O Holy and Ever-Blessed Trinity, Father, Son and Holy Ghost.

THOU art worthy to receive glory and honor and power. . . Blessing, honor, glory and power be unto Him That sitteth upon the Throne, and to the Lamb, for ever and ever. Amen.

FORGIVE, O Lord, I most humbly implore Thee, my many sins, and be gracious to my great unworthiness, granting me Thy blessing and grace so to minister before Thee as will wholly show forth Thy praise and be to the good of souls: through. . .

Before the Holy Gospel.

O LORD and Lover of men, cause the pure Light of Thy divine knowledge to shine forth in our hearts, and open the eyes of our understanding, that we may comprehend the precepts of Thy Gospel; plant in us also the fear of Thy blessed commandments, that we, trampling upon all carnal lusts, may seek a heavenly citizenship, both saying and doing always such things as shall well please Thee; for Thou art the illumination of our souls and bodies, Christ our God; and to Thee we ascribe. . .

After the Holy Gospel.

O GOD, Who hast sounded into our ears Thy divine and salutary oracles; Illuminate the souls of us sinners to the comprehension of that which has been read, so that we may not only be seen to be hearers of spiritual things, but doers of good works, following after faith without guile, blameless life, conversation without charge of guilt; in Christ Jesus our Lord, with Whom Thou art blessed, with Thy most Holy and Good and Quickening Spirit, now and ever and to ages of ages.

Before Preaching.

O LORD JESUS, Who hast done all things well, Who makest both the deaf to hear and the dumb to speak: I beseech Thee, lay Thy hands upon me, loose the string of my tongue, that I may speak plain; open the deaf ears of Thy people, that they may hear the words which belong unto eternal life; Who livest. . .

A LMIGHTY and everlasting God, the source and perfection of all virtues: Grant me, I beseech Thee, both to do what is right, and to preach what is true: that both by action and teaching I may afford to Thy faithful people the instruction which is of Thy grace; through. . .

I N the humility of my spirit do I approach Thee, Who hast given unto me hope and spiritual strength; do Thou, therefore, O Son of David, Who hast come to us in the flesh, revealed in mystery, open, with the key of Thy cross, the secrets of my heart, sending one of the seraphim, who with a burning coal, taken from Thine altar on high, may purify my unclean lips: O enlighten my mind that I may minister in love to the edification of the hearer, and may not give occasion of error, but be ever a preacher of eternal truth; through Thee, O my God, Who livest. . .

On Entering the Pulpit.
IN the Name. . .

O LORD, open Thou my lips: and my mouth shall show forth Thy praise.

LET the words of my mouth and the meditation of my heart be acceptable in Thy sight, O Lord, my Strength and my Redeemer.

ALL glory be to the Father, and to the Son, and to the Holy Ghost. Amen.

After Preaching.
IN Thy Name, O God, I, Thy humble servant, have sown Thy seed; do Thou give the increase, to the health of souls, the spread of Thy kingdom and Thy glory. All glory and honor be unto Thee, O God. Amen.

Before the Holy Communion.
O GOD, be merciful to me, the sinner.

O HOLY GHOST, sanctify us and purify my heart and lips, that in the Name of the Lord and in the power of His Word, I

may worthily administer this holy sacrament;
Who with. . .

WE RENDER Thee thanks, O Lord our
God, that Thou hast given us boldness
to enter into the Holiest, through the Blood
of Jesus, by the new and living Way Which
Thou hast consecrated through the veil of
flesh of Thy Christ; therefore, thus entering
into the tabernacle of Thy glory and brought
within the veil, we fall down before Thee,
full of fear and dread. . . but Thou, O Lord,
send forth Thy grace, and hallow our souls,
bodies and spirits, that so with pure hearts
we may offer to Thee this sacrifice of praise
and thanksgiving; through the Same. . .

O GOD, Who makest the unworthy worthy,
sinners righteous, impure pure: Cleanse
my soul and body of all shame and sin and
make me a worthy and watchful servant at
Thy holy altar. Graciously grant me to bring
before Thee acceptable and well-pleasing sac-
rifices in true repentance for my sins and
misdeeds, for my daily, countless transgressions. To a like worthiness prepare all who
this day approach Thy sacrament (especially
those who have asked my prayers); and may
this sacrifice of our broken and contrite spirits and hearts be acceptable to Thee through

Him Who offered Himself to Thee, O God
Father, the perfect propitiatory Sacrifice,
Who is our sinless and only Mediator, through
the High Priest, Jesus Christ, Thy dear Son.

COUNT us worthy of this communion also,
O God of Truth, and make our bodies to
contain purity and our souls prudence and
knowledge; and make us wise, O God of Com-
passions, by the participation of the body and
blood, because through Thy Only-Begotten to
Thee is glory and strength in the Holy Spirit,
now and to all the ages of the ages. Amen.

WE do not presume to come to this Thy
table, O merciful Lord, trusting in our
own righteousness, but in Thy manifold and
great mercies: We be not worthy so much as
to gather up the crumbs under Thy table; but
Thou art the same Lord, Whose property is
always to have mercy; grant us therefore,
gracious Lord, so to eat the Flesh of Thy
dear Son, and to drink His blood in these
holy mysteries, that we may continually dwell
in Him and He in us, that our sinful bodies
may be made clean by His body, and our souls
washed through His most precious blood.

CREATOR of all things invisible and
visible, Thou Who guardest all things
with Thy Providence, for all things are

Thine: O Lord, Thou Friend of souls, I, miserable, unworthy servant, cry unto Thee, the Almighty Lord, because I approach Thy sanctuary and am about to stretch forth my hands to administer Thy Holy Sacrament. Give me, O Lord, Thy Holy Spirit, the Heavenly Fire, Who passeth all understanding, softeneth all hardness of heart, wipeth out every evil thought and quieteth all unrest of the soul with its sorrow and pain; and grant, that I, as is meet in Thy steward, may be raised up over every earthly and mortal thought; and that pure in heart and mouth, I may fulfill this most holy and mystery-filled Word, in communion with Thy Christ, Who. . .

LORD, I am not worthy that Thou shouldst come under my roof, for it is desolate and ruinous, neither wilt Thou find within me place to lay Thy head; but since Thou hast not disdained to recline in a stable with the brute beasts, nor disdained to be the guest of Simon the Leper, neither hast spurned the woman, who like me, was a great sinner, nor abhorred the washing of her tears: So deign, O Lord, to receive me, the chief of sinners, to the participation of This immaculate and life-giving sacrament.

TRUSTING only in Thy mercy, O Lord, Jesus, I draw near: sick that Thou mayest heal me, hungry that Thou mayest feed me, thirsty that Thou mayest give me drink, poor and needy that Thou mayest relieve me, desolate to my kind Comforter.

But whence is this to me that Thou shouldest come unto me and give Thyself to me? How shall I appear before Thee, how canst Thou come to me a sinner?

Thou knowest, O good Lord, that I have no good thing in me to deserve this mercy: I confess my unworthiness, I acknowledge Thy goodness, I give Thee thanks for Thy mercy, I praise Thee for Thine exceeding love.

Since, therefore, it is Thy will, since Thou hast said, "Come unto Me," I come, O Lord; let not my sins move Thee to reject me; be it unto me according to Thy Word; for there is none other Name under heaven given among men whereby we must be saved, but Thine, O most blessed Lord and Saviour.

And whatsoever is wanting unto me, do Thou, O most merciful Jesus, vouchsafe to supply out of the riches of Thy merits, Thy pains and labors, Thy bitter death, whereby Thou hast redeemed me, Who livest and reignest with. . .

O LORD, all that is in heaven and earth is Thine. I would, in full surrender and complete joy, offer myself, a sacrifice, to Thee, and ever remain Thine. O Lord, with upright heart, I consecrate myself to Thee this day, to a constant service, to obedience and as an offering of constant love and praise. Receive me at this Holy Supper; and as Thou art there present, unite Thyself through the same with me and with the company of Thy believers that it may serve them and me to our souls' health; Who. . .

O LORD JESUS CHRIST, Thou Only-begotten Son of the living God, eternal High Priest, Who hast given Thy body in bitter death for us all, and hast shed Thy blood for the forgiveness of our sins, and now givest us this very body and blood in the blessed Sacrament, commanding us to eat and drink in memory of Thy death: We bring before Thy Divine majesty these Thy gifts, bread and wine, and pray that according to Thy Word, through Thy grace, goodness and power, Thou wouldest sanctify, bless and use them that this bread be Thy body and this wine Thy blood, that all who in true faith, and with contrite hearts, eat and drink thereof, may be blessed unto eternal Life; Who livest. . .

An Epiklesis.

O GOD of truth, let Thy holy Word come upon this bread that the bread may become the body of the Word, and upon this cup that the cup may become the blood of the Truth; and make all who communicate to receive a medicine of life for the healing of every sickness and for the strengthening of all advancement and virtue, not for condemnation, O God of truth, and not for censure and reproach. For we have invoked Thee, the Uncreated, through the Only-Begotten in the Holy Spirit.

An Epiklesis.

SEND down upon us also, and upon this bread and upon these cups, Thy Holy Spirit, that by His all-powerful and Divine influence He may sanctify and consecrate them, and make this bread the body, and this cup the blood of the New Testament, of the very Lord and God and Saviour and universal King, Christ Jesus. That to all of us who partake thereof they may tend unto faith, sobriety, healing, temperance, sanctification, the renewal of soul, body and spirit, participation in the blessedness of eternal life and immortality, the glory of Thy most holy name, and the remission of sins, that Thy

most holy, precious and glorious Name may
be praised and glorified in this, as in all
things.

At the Consecration.

ONE Holy, One Lord, one Jesus Christ to
the glory of God the Father, blessed for
evermore. Amen. Glory be to God in the
Highest, and on earth peace to men of good
will. Hosannah to the Son of David. Blessed
is He Who cometh in the Name of the Lord:
God is the Lord, and He hath appeared unto
us. Hosannah in the Highest.

Before Communing.

O GOD the FATHER in heaven, have
mercy upon me, be gracious unto me
Thy child, who in childlike fear, am about
to approach Thy holy altar. Let me partake
of Thy heavenly feast, as Thou hast prepared
it for me, to the salvation of my soul.

O GOD the SON, SAVIOUR of the world,
have mercy upon me, and let me be a
loving guest at Thy holy supper. Give me
what Thou hast promised and let me take
what Thou hast appointed for me.

O GOD the HOLY GHOST, have mercy upon me, be gracious unto me, and grant that I receive this holy sacrament worthily, that through it my weak faith may be strengthened, my cold heart kindled with love, my troubled conscience comforted, my hope freshened, my sinful life bettered, and finally be saved.

O LORD help me. Amen.

O LORD JESUS, I am not worthy that Thou shouldest enter my sinful heart, but Thou knowest my great poverty and need. I long for Thy presence with all my heart, therefore, feed, comfort, strengthen my poor soul; Who livest. . .

On Receiving the Bread.

GLORY be to Thee, O Lord Jesus Christ! Welcome to my soul, Lord Jesus, with the precious food of Thy most holy body, which, with the consecrated bread, Thou now givest me to eat in Thy sacrament, as Thou gavest it for me in Thy bitter death on the cross, for the forgiveness of my sins. May this bless me unto everlasting life. Amen.

On Receiving the Wine.

GLORY be to Thee, O Lord Jesus Christ! Welcome to my soul, Lord Jesus, with the precious drink of Thy most holy blood, which, with the consecrated wine, Thou givest me to drink in Thy sacrament, as Thou didst pour it out on the cross for the forgiveness of my sins. May this bless me into everlasting life. Amen.

Or:

HAIL, most holy body of Christ! blessed Jesus be Thou to me, the sinner, Life, Health and Salvation: be Thou my food, my consolation now, and at the hour of my death. Amen.

HAIL, most precious blood of my Saviour, washing away all sin! Most loving Jesus, do Thou cleanse, sanctify and preserve my soul, to everlasting life. Amen.

Or:

GLORY be to Thee, O Lord, Who feedest me with the bread of life! O Lord God, Who didst sanctify us by the offering of the body of Jesus once for all, sanctify me. . . even me, O heavenly Father. Amen.

GLORY be to Thee, O Lord Jesus, Who permittest me to drink of the fountain of life freely!

Thou hast loved us and washed us from our sins in Thine own blood. To Thee be glory and dominion for ever and ever. Amen.

Thanksgiving after the Communion.

GLORY be to Thee, my Lord and my God, for thus feeding me with Thy most blessed body and blood! Let This heavenly food impart new life and vigor to me, and to all who communicate with me, that our faith may increase daily, that we may become humble and contrite for our sins, may love Thee, serve Thee, delight in Thee, and praise Thee, more fervently and constantly than we have ever done before; O Thou, Who with...

WE give thanks unto Thee, O God, even we who are sunken in so many sins and have found no health and comfort save that which is with Thee only: We humbly beseech Thee that Thou wilt not turn from us, though it be but our just desert, the light of Thy countenance, but according to Thy great mercy increase in us continually that which Thou hast already begun; through. . .

Concerning the Eucharist, thus give thanks:

FIRST as to the cup: We give Thee thanks, our Father, for the Holy Vine of David, Thy servant, Which Thou hast made known to us through Jesus, Thy Servant; to Thee be the glory unto the ages.

As to the broken bread: We give thanks, our Father, for the life and the knowledge which Thou hast made known unto us through Jesus, Thy Servant; to Thee be the glory unto the ages. As this broken bread was scattered over the hills, and having been gathered, became one, so may Thy Church be gathered, from the ends of the earth into Thy Kingdom; for Thine is the glory and power through Jesus Christ unto the ages.

THOU hast given unto us, O Lord, sanctification in the communion of the all-holy body and precious blood of Thy Only-Begotten Son, our Lord Jesus Christ; give unto us also the grace of Thy Good Spirit, and keep us blameless in the faith, lead us into perfect adoption and redemption, and to the coming joys of eternity; for Thou art our sanctification and light, O God, and Thy Only-Begotten Son, and Thy All-Holy Spirit, now and ever and unto the ages. Amen.

AH, Jesus, what canst Thou refuse me, when Thou hast given me Thyself—and where is the confidence that can be too tender? Why should I envy Thy beloved disciple who leaned on Thy breast at Thy last supper? For dost Thou not at present rest in my heart? O let me, then, be forever inviolably attached to Thee! Let the sweets of Thy presence so captivate my soul, that disgusted with sin, it may be fixed in the contemplation of Thee, and ever listen with ready obedience to Thy holy inspiration; Who livest. . .

FINISHED and accomplished as far as in us lieth, O Christ, our God, is the mystery of Thy dispensation; for we have had the memorial of Thy death, we have seen the figure of Thy resurrection, we have been filled with Thine imperishable life, we have had delight in Thy delicacies, in which there is no satiety, and which do Thou be pleased to award to us all in the world to come, by the grace of Thine eternal Father, and of the holy, good, and life-giving Spirit, now and ever, and unto the ages of ages.

Before the Benediction.

I STRETCH out the hand upon this people and pray that the hand of the truth may be stretched out and blessing given to this

people on account of Thy lovingkindness, O
God of compassion:—May a hand of piety
and power and sound discipline and cleanness
and all holiness, bless this people, and continually preserve it to advancement and im-
provement, through Thy Only-Begotten Jesus
Christ in the Holy Spirit. . .

After the Benediction.

GLORY be to the Father, and to the Son,
and to the Holy Ghost: as it was in the
beginning, is now, and ever shall be, world
without end. Amen.

GOING on from strength to strength, and
having fulfilled all the Divine service in
Thy temple, even now we beseech Thee, Lord
our God, make us worthy of perfect loving-
kindness, make straight our path, root us in
Thy fear, and make us worthy of the heavenly
Kingdom, in Christ Jesus our Lord, with
Whom Thou art blessed, together with Thy
all-holy and good and quickening Spirit, now
and always and unto the ages. Amen.

GRANT, O Lord, that as I have now cele-
brated Thy worship (and received Thy
holy sacrament), so I may likewise, by Thy
grace, do honor to Thee in all my daily life;
through. . .

O GOD, the life of the faithful, the bliss the righteous: Mercifully receive the prayers of Thy suppliants that the souls which thirst for Thy promises may evermore be filled from Thine abundance; through. . .

O LORD, we beseech Thee, grant to Thy Christian people at last to know what now they confess, and to see in perfect love the heavenly gift whereof they oft partake; through. . .

After the Service in the Sacristy.

MOST BLESSED LORD JESUS, that which Thou hast commanded, I have done, I did it in weakness, for I am a poor sinner; nevertheless, in obedience to Thy Word and command, this holy work has been finished. Therefore Thy blessing will not be lacking to those who have received Thy body and blood in faith.

I humbly worship Thee, and commit to Thy gracious keeping all these souls which Thou hast lately fed with Thy precious gifts through my ministry; and beseech Thee that Thou wouldest guard and keep them in Thy grace and love that they may be further strengthened and built up until Thou dost finally take them to Thy heavenly feast.

To Thee be all glory and majesty unto the ages of ages. Amen.

O LORD God Almighty, mercifully accept this our service, and grant that we, striving to do Thy will on earth as it is done in heaven, may there with Thy holy angels ever praise Thy blessed name; through. . .

FORGIVE for Christ's sake, O merciful Father, the imperfections of this service, and grant that our lives may show forth Thy praise. Amen.

On Leaving the Church.

THE LORD preserve my going out and coming in from this time forth and for evermore. Amen.

GLORY be to the Father. . .

Before and after Vespers.

JESUS, Master, do Thou meet us while we walk in the way, and long to reach the heavenly country, so that following Thy light, we may keep the way of righteousness, and never wander away into the horrible darkness of this world's night, while Thou, Who art the Way, the Truth, and the Life, art shining within us; Who livest. . .

IN Thy most holy name, O God, Father, Son and Holy Ghost, I began my sacred work and service this day; under Thy blessing I have performed it; and through Thy power completed it. May it be to the eternal blessing of my congregation and myself. Graciously receive my humble sacrifice of praise for Thy rich help and mercy. Unto Thee alone, all honor, glory, and praise, unto the ages of ages. Amen.

LITANIES

LITANY FOR MATINS.

GLORY be to Thee, O Lord, glory to Thee.

Glory to Thee, Who givest me sleep, to recruit my weakness, and to remit the toils of this fretful flesh.

To this day, and all days, a perfect, holy, peaceful, healthy, sinless course,

Vouchsafe, O Lord.

The angel of peace, a faithful guide, guardian of souls and bodies, to encamp around me, and ever to prompt what is salutary,

Vouchsafe, O Lord.

Pardon and remission of all sins and all offences,

Vouchsafe, O Lord.

To our souls what is good and convenient, and peace to the world,

Vouchsafe, O Lord.

Whatever is true, whatever is honest, whatever is just, whatever pure, whatever lovely, whatever of good report, if there be any virtue, if any praise, such thoughts, such deeds,

Vouchsafe, O Lord.

A Christian close, without sin, without shame, and, should it please Thee, without pain, and a good answer at the dreadful and fearful judgment seat of Jesus Christ, our Lord,

Vouchsafe, O Lord.

AMEN.

LITANY OF THE MOST HOLY NAME
OF JESUS

LORD, have mercy upon us.
  Christ, have mercy upon us.
Lord, have mercy upon us.

O Jesus, hear us.
  O Jesus, hear us.

O GOD, the Father in Heaven,
  Have mercy upon us.
O GOD, the Son, Redeemer of the world,
  Have mercy upon us.
O GOD, the Holy Ghost,
  Have mercy upon us.
O Holy Trinity, One God,
  Have mercy upon us.

JESUS, Son of the living God,
Jesus, Splendor of the Father,
Jesus, Brightness of eternal
  light,
Jesus, King of glory,
Jesus, Sun of righteousness,
Jesus, Most admirable,
Jesus, Most delectable,

} Have mercy upon us.

Jesus, Strength of God,
Jesus, Patron of the future ages,
Jesus, Counsel of the mighty
  angels,
Jesus, most powerful,
Jesus, most patient,
Jesus, most obedient,
Jesus, most gentle,
Jesus, most loving,
Jesus, our Lover.

} Have mercy upon us.

JESUS, Peace of GOD,
Jesus, Author of life,
Jesus, Pattern of virtues,
Jesus, Lover of souls,
Jesus, our God,
Jesus, our refuge,
Jesus, Father of the poor,
Jesus, Treasure of the faithful,
Jesus, Good Shepherd,
Jesus, True Light,
Jesus, Eternal Wisdom,
Jesus, Infinite Good,
Jesus, our Way and Life,
Jesus, Joy of the angels,
Jesus, King of the patriarchs,
Jesus, Master of the apostles,
Jesus, Teacher of the evan-
  gelists,

} Have mercy upon us.

Jesus, Courage of the martyrs,
Jesus, Light of the confessors,
Jesus, Crown of the saints: } Have mercy upon us.

Be merciful,
    Spare us, O Jesus.
Be merciful,
    Hear us, O Jesus.

From all evil,
From all sin,
From Thy wrath,
From the snares of the devil,
From everlasting death: } Deliver us, O Jesus.

Through the mystery of Thy
    incarnation,
Through Thy nativity,
Through Thy infancy,
Through Thy most holy life,
Through Thy woes,
Through Thy agony and passion
Through Thy cross and languor.
Through Thy death and burial,
Through Thy resurrection,
Through Thy ascension,
Through Thy joys,
Through Thy glory: } Deliver us, O Jesus.

O Lamb of God, that takest away the sin of
the world;
Have mercy upon us.
O Lamb of God, that takest away the sin of
the world;
Have mercy upon us.
O Lamb of God, that takest away the sin of
the world;
Grant us Thy peace.

O Jesus, hear us.
O Jesus, hear us.

LORD, have mercy upon us.
Christ, have mercy upon us.
Lord, have mercy upon us.

OUR Father, Who art in Heaven. . .

V: Blessed be the Name of the Lord.
R: From this time forth and for evermore.

O LORD, make us to have equally a perpetual fear and love of Thy holy name, because Thou never leavest those destitute of
Thy governance, whom Thou hast founded in
the steadfastness of Thy love; through. . .

V: I will praise the name of God,
R: And will magnify Him with thanksgiving.

O LORD, JESUS CHRIST, Who hast said: Ask and ye shall receive, seek and ye shall find, knock and it shall be opened to you: Grant to us now asking, we beseech Thee, the true affection of Thy most holy name, that we may love Thee with our whole heart, mouth and in all our work, and never cease from Thy praise; Who livest. . .

V: God hath highly exalted Him,
R: And given Him a name which is above every name.

O GOD, Who hast made the name of Jesus Christ, Thy Son, our Lord, most dear to Thy faithful people, and most terrible to the evil spirits: Grant, we beseech Thee, that all we who worship This name on earth, may receive in this life the sweetness of Thy holy consolations, and in the world to come, the joy of exaltation, and of eternal blessedness in heaven; through the same Jesus Christ, our Lord, who liveth. . .

LITANY OF THE PASSION

LORD, have mercy upon us,
 Christ, have mercy upon us.
Lord, have mercy upon us.

O GOD, the Father in heaven,
 Have mercy upon us.
O God, the Son, Redeemer of the world,
 Have mercy upon us.
O God, the Holy Ghost,
 Have mercy upon us.
O Holy Trinity, One God,
 Have mercy upon us.

JESUS, Son of the living God,
 Have mercy upon us.

From all evil,
 O Jesus, deliver us.

From sudden, unprepared or evil
 death,
From the snares of the devil,
From anger, hatred or ill-will,
From everlasting death:

O Jesus, deliver us.

By the mystery of Thy incarnation,

By Thy most holy life and conversation,

By Thy most bitter passion and death,

By Thine agony and bloody sweat,

By Thy thrice repeated prayer,

By Thy bonds and stripes,

By Thy sacred body buffeted and smitten,

By the spitting upon Thy adorable face,

By the false judgment pronounced on Thee by Caiaphas,

By Thy being set at nought by Herod,

By the shameful stripping off of Thy garments,

By Thy painful crown of thorns,

By Thy purple robe of mockery,

By Thy most unjust condemnation,

By Thy bearing Thine own cross,

By Thy footprints traced in blood,

By the tearing off of Thy garments,

By the cruel straining of Thy sacred limbs,

By Thy dread crucifixion,

By the up-raising of Thy cross,

O Jesus, deliver us.

By the anguish which Thou didst suffer,
By the insults which Thou didst endure,
By Thy prayers and tears,
By the shedding of Thy most precious blood,
By Thy patience and humility,
By the love wherewith Thou didst love us to the end:

O Jesus, deliver us.

We sinners beseech Thee to hear us:
O most loving Jesus.

That being dead unto sin, we may live unto righteousness,
That we may not glory, save in the cross of our Lord Jesus Christ,
That we may take our cross daily and follow Thee,
That Thy blood may cleanse us from dead works to serve the living God,
That looking unto Thy example, we may follow Thy steps,
That being partakers of Thy sufferings, we may be also of Thy glory:

We beseech Thee to hear us, O Jesus.

O Lamb of God, that takest away the sin of
    the world;
        Have mercy upon us.
O Lamb of God, that takest away the sin of
    the world;
        Have mercy upon us.
O Lamb of God, that takest away the sin of
    the world;
        Grant us Thy Peace.

V: We adore Thee, we bless Thee, O Jesus.
R: Because by Thy cross and passion Thou
    hast redeemed the world.

O LORD, JESUS CHRIST, Son of the liv-
    ing GOD, Who at the sixth hour was
lifted upon the cross for the redemption of the
world, and didst shed Thy blood for the remission of our sins: We humbly beseech Thee
that, by the virtue and merits of Thy most
holy life, passion and death, Thou wouldst
grant us to enter into the gates of paradise
with joy; Who livest. . .

LITANY OF THE HOLY SACRAMENT

L ORD, have mercy upon us.
    Christ, have mercy upon us.
Lord, have mercy upon us.

O GOD, the Father in heaven,
    Have mercy upon us.
O God, the Son, Redeemer of the world,
    Have mercy upon us.
O God, the Holy Ghost,
    Have mercy upon us.
O Holy Trinity, One God,
    Have mercy upon us.

LIVING Bread, Which camest
  down from heaven,
Hidden God and Saviour,
Perpetual Sacrifice,
Pure Oblation,
Lamb without spot,
Food of angels,
Hidden Manna,
Daily Bread,
Word made flesh and dwelling
  in us,
Bread of life,
Cup of blessing:
} Have mercy upon us.

Mystery of the faith,
Fulness of Divine love,
Medicine of immortality,
Bread made flesh by the power
   of the word,
Priest and Victim,   } Have mercy
Hope of penitents,   upon us.
Refreshment of holy souls,
Food by the way for those who
   die in the faith,
Pledge of glory in the life to
   come:

Be merciful unto us.
   Spare us, good Lord.

Be merciful unto us.
   Hear us, good Lord.

From unworthy reception of Thy body and
   blood:
   Good Lord, deliver us.

From the lust of the flesh,
From the lust of the eye,   } Good Lord,
From the pride of life,   deliver us.
From all occasions of sin:

By the deep humility with which Thou didst wash the disciples' feet,

By that great love with which Thou didst institute this holy sacrament,

By Thy most sacred body and precious blood, which Thou hast left us in the sacrament of the altar,

By the wounds which Thou receivedst for us, and by Thy death upon the cross:

Good Lord, deliver us.

We poor sinners do beseech Thee,
To hear us, O Lord God.

That it may please Thee to preserve in us faith, reverence and devotion, with regard to this wonderful sacrament,

That it . . . . to forgive us for having received it at any time without due preparation,

That it . . . . to bring us by a true confession of our sins to a frequent and worthy use of this holy sacrament,

We beseech Thee to hear us, good Lord.

That it . . . . to grant unto us
  the precious and heavenly
  fruits of this most holy
  sacrament,

That it . . . . to comfort and
  defend us in the hour of our
  death, with this heavenly
  food for our journey:

We beseech Thee to hear us, good Lord.

SON OF GOD,
  We beseech Thee to hear us.

O Lamb of God . . . . .
  . . . . . Grant us Thy Peace.

Lord, have mercy upon us. . . . .

OUR FATHER, Who art in Heaven. . . . .

V: Bless the Lord, O my soul,
R: And all that is within me, bless His holy
  name.

O LORD GOD, Who hast left unto us in a
    wonderful sacrament a memorial of Thy
passion: Grant, we beseech Thee, that we may
so use this sacrament of Thy body and blood,
that the fruits of Thy redemption may continually be manifest in us; Who livest. . . . .

LITANY OF THE HOLY GHOST

L ORD, have mercy upon us.
Christ, have mercy upon us.
Lord, have mercy upon us.

O GOD, the Father in heaven,
Have mercy upon us.
O God, the Son, Redeemer of the world,
Have mercy upon us.
O God, the Holy Ghost,
Have mercy upon us.
O Holy Trinity, One God,
Have mercy upon us.

O HOLY GHOST, by Whose wondrous power the incarnation of our Lord was wrought in the Virgin's womb,

O Holy Ghost, Who teachest us all things, and guidest us into all truth,

O Holy Ghost, Who makest intercessions for us with groanings that cannot be uttered,

Have mercy upon us.

O Holy Ghost, by Whom we
are born again and made
heirs of eternal life,
O Holy Ghost, Who helpest
our infirmities,
O Holy Ghost, Who quickenest
us, and purifiest our hearts
by faith,
O Holy Ghost, Who art a dis-
cerner of the thoughts and
intents of the heart:

} Have mercy upon us.

From all evil,
Deliver us, O Holy Ghost.
Be merciful unto us,
Spare us, O Holy Ghost.
Be merciful unto us,
Hear us, O Holy Ghost.

From all sins of thought, word
and deed,
From the crafts and assaults
of the devil,
From presumption and despair,
From unbelief and hardness of
heart,
From uncleanness of heart and
life,
From anger, hatred and ill-
will,

} Deliver us, O Holy Ghost

From impurity of body and soul,
From obstinacy and impenitence,
From indifference in the service of God: } Deliver us, O Holy Ghost.

Thou Who procedest from the Father and the Son,
Thou Who didst overshadow the Virgin,
Thou Who descendest upon the Son of God in the form of a dove,
Thou Who wast poured out upon the holy apostles,
Thou Spirit of love,
Thou Spirit of joy,
Thou Spirit of peace,
Thou Who dwellest in us: } Help us, Good Lord.

By Thine invisible anointing,
By the abundance of Thy grace, } Hear us, Good Lord.

We sinners do beseech Thee,
To hear us, O Holy Ghost.

That Thou wouldest cleanse and sanctify all the members of Thy holy Church,

That Thou wouldest adorn the Bride of Christ with manifold gifts,

That Thou wouldest bless and protect our synod, together with all its clergy and institutions,

That Thou wouldest grant us all the spirit of prayer and reverent worship,

That Thou wouldest adorn our lives with p a t i e n c e and humility,

That Thou wouldest kindle in us love and mercy,

That Thou wouldest clothe us with chastity,

That Thou wouldest help us that we grieve Thee not, O Holy Ghost, whereby we are sealed unto the day of redemption,

That Thou wouldest work in us Thy grace and bring us to everlasting life:

We beseech Thee to hear us, O Holy Ghost.

O Lord God, the Holy Ghost,
      Have mercy upon us.

O Lamb of God, that takest away the sin
    of the world;
      Have mercy upon us.
O Lamb of God, that takest away the sin
    of the world;
      Have mercy upon us.
O Lamb of God, that takest away the sin
    of the world;
      Grant us Thy Peace.

O Christ hear us,
      O Christ hear us.

Lord, have mercy upon us.
Christ, have mercy upon us.
Lord, have mercy upon us.

OUR FATHER, Who art in Heaven. . .

V: Create in me a clean heart O God.
R: And renew a right spirit within me.

SEND, I beseech Thee, Almighty God, the
Holy Ghost, into my heart, that He may
rule and direct me according to Thy will,
comfort me in all my temptations and af-

flictions, defend me from all error, and lead
me into all truth, that I, being steadfast in
the true faith, may increase in love and in all
good works and in the end obtain everlasting
life; through. . .

LITANY OF INTERCESSION

LORD, have mercy upon us.
  Lord, have mercy upon us.
Christ, have mercy upon us.
  Christ have mercy upon us.
Lord, have mercy upon us.
  Lord, have mercy upon us.

O GOD, the Father in Heaven:
  Have mercy upon us.
O God, the Son, Redeemer of the world:
  Have mercy upon us.
O Holy Trinity, One God:
  Have mercy upon us.

O God, Whose ear is open to our prayer:
  Graciously regard *those* for whom we offer
    our supplications.

O Christ, hear us.
  O Christ, hear us.

From all evil: ⎫
From all sin: ⎭ Good Lord, deliver *them*.

From the crafts and assaults
  of the devil;
From the   temptations   and
  lusts of the flesh;
From loneliness and despair;
From carelessness and forget-
  fulness of duty;
From loss of courage and
  devotion;
From making shipwreck of
  their faith;
And from falling away from
  Thee:

} Good Lord,
deliver *them.*

By Thy coming to save man-
  kind;
By Thy selfless service;
By Thy love to the weary and
  heavy laden;
By Thy healing touch to the
  sick;
By Thy word of invitation to
  all;
By Thy w e l c o m e   to   the
  sinner;
By Thy cross and passion;
By Thy victory;
By the might of Thy salva-
  tion;
O Lover of men:

} Help, *them,*
good Lord.

In all time of *their* tribula-
   tion;
In *their* hour of need;
In *their* hour of death;
And in the day of judgment:
} Help *them,*
good Lord.

We poor sinners do beseech Thee:
   To hear us, O Lord God.

And to grant *them* Thy guidance and pro-
   tection;
To keep *them* pure in thought, word and
   deed;
To guard *their* lives and souls;
To make *them* valiant soldiers of the cross;
To hold *them* steadfast in *their* allegiance to
   our country;
To be *their* Protection in danger;
To be *their* Refreshment in hardship;
To be *their* Comfort in suffering;
To be *their* Companion in the weary and
   lonely hours;
To make *them* gentle and lovers of *their*
   fellowmen;
And in the hours of trial, keep Thou *them*
   in the hollow of Thy hand:
     We humbly beseech Thee to hear us,
      good Lord.

To preserve our country at all times, whether
   times of peril, peace or prosperity;

To direct and protect our President, his counsellors, and all in authority;

To foster in our hearts reverence for the Law
   of our Land;

To uphold our army and navy;

To grant victory to every righteous cause, for
   which our nation is contending;

To weld our nation as one in loyalty and
   faithful devotion;

And to turn all mankind to Thy cross and to
   fill all hearts with love for Thee:

     We humbly beseech Thee to hear us,
       good Lord.

To behold and succor all who are in danger,
   necessity and tribulation;

To protect all who travel by land or water;

To comfort and heal the wounded;

To mitigate and shorten the pains of the
   dying;

To set free the captives;

To protect and provide for all fatherless and
   widows;

To overthrow man's inhumanity to man;

To bless and strengthen all who are ministering to their fellowmen;

And to have mercy upon all men:
>   We humbly beseech Thee to hear us,
>   good Lord.

To forgive our enemies;
To turn their hearts that they may cease their
   enmity;
To incline their hearts and ours that we may
   walk together in meekness and peace;
To restore speedily to all nations just and
   lasting peace;
And graciously to hear our prayers:
>   We beseech Thee to hear us, good Lord.

O Lord, Jesus Christ, Son of God:
>   We beseech Thee to hear us.

O Lamb of God, That takest away the sin
   of the world;
>   Have mercy upon us.
O Lamb of God, That takest away the sin
   of the world;
>   Have mercy upon us.
O Lamb of God, That takest away the sin
   of the world;
>   Grant us Thy peace.

O Christ, hear us.
>   O Christ, hear us.

Lord, have mercy upon us.
> Lord, have mercy upon us.
Christ, have mercy upon us.
> Christ, have mercy upon us.
Lord, have mercy upon us.
> Lord, have mercy upon us.

OUR FATHER, Who art in heaven. . .

Let us humble ourselves before God, let us implore the Father Almighty:

Who graciously heareth those who call upon Him and forsaketh not those who trust in Him.

OH how great is Thy compassion, O Lord: in that Thou succorest the captives, pitiest the wretched and afflicted, art indulgent to sinners, comfortest those driven hither and yon, raisest up the oppressed, hearest the praying: To those who have not, give! grant forgiveness to sinners: convert the peoples to calling on and honoring Thy Name; put in our hearts that mercy which Thou, O Holy and Merciful God, showerest on us; and hear our prayers through the merits of Thy Son, Jesus Christ, our Lord. Amen.

Let us carry before the throne of mercy our needy brethren:

That He Whose love never faileth, may grant them His blessing.

O LORD, look down from heaven, behold, visit and relieve Thy servants for whom we offer our supplications; look upon them with the eyes of Thy mercy; give them comfort and sure confidence in Thee; defend them from the danger of the enemy; and keep them in perpetual peace and safety; through Jesus Christ, Thy Son, our Lord. Amen.

Let us pray our Lord, the Prince of Peace, to establish His reign in every heart:

That His Kingdom may come and His will be done.

ETERNAL Father, Who in the sending of Thy Son, Jesus Christ, our Lord, didst speak Peace to the world, and in the blood of His Cross hast opened the way to all mankind to find peace with and in Thee: Hold Thou the Cross high that every eye may see, fire every heart with Thy Spirit that all may accept in Christ the way of life, that following His holy example and burning with His zeal of service, all mankind may be one brotherhood in Him, and Thy peace possess every heart and rule in all the nations of the world, through the same Jesus Christ, our Lord, Who. . . Amen.

LITANY FOR THE SICK

L ORD GOD, the Father in Heaven,
     Have mercy upon *him.*
Lord God, the Son, Redeemer of the world,
  Have mercy upon *him.*
Lord God, the Holy Ghost,
  Have mercy upon *him.*

     Be gracious to *him.*
          Spare *him,* good Lord.

     Be gracious to *him.*
          Help *him,* good Lord.

     From all sin,
          Good Lord, deliver *him.*

From all unbelief and doubt,
From Thy just and dreadful
  wrath,
From the crafts and assaults
  of the devil,   Defend *him,*
From the fear of eternal   good Lord.
  death,
From the anguish and pains of
  hell,
And from all evil:

By Thy holy nativity,
By Thine agony and bloody
  sweat,
By Thy cross and passion,
By Thy glorious resurrection
  and ascension: } Help *him*, O Lord God.

In the hour of death,
And in the day of Judgment: } Help *him*, good Lord.

We poor sinners beseech Thee:
    To hear us, O Lord God.

That Thou wouldest give *him*
  health of body and soul;
That *he* may confidently look
  to Thy fatherly goodness for
  whatsoever is needful;
That *he* may be enabled to call
  upon Thee in true faith;
That Thy good angel may
  defend, direct and conduct
  him in all *his* ways;
That, in steadfast faith, *he*
  may withstand and over-
  come all temptation;
That *he* may resign himself,
  body and soul, to Thy will;
That *he* may truly know and
  heartily repent of all *his*
  sins;   } Hear us, good Lord.

That *he* may find comfort in
  Thy goodness and mercy;
That *he* may willingly forgive
  all *his* enemies and per-
  secutors;
That *he* may turn away from
  all lusts and pleasures of the
  world;
That *his* desire may be unto
  Thee and the treasures of
  Thy heavenly kingdom;
That *he* may await *his* last
  hour in patience;
That *he* may commit *his* spirit
  into Thy hands;
That *his* departure may be in
  peace;
That *he* may have part in the
  resurrection unto life;
That *he* may meet *his* Lord
  with joy;
That *he* may live for ever i
  Thy kingdom:

} Hear us,
good Lord.

O Lord Jesus Christ, Son of God;
     Have mercy upon *him.*

O Lamb of God, that takest away the sin
    of the world;
     Have mercy upon *him.*

O Lamb of God, that takest away the sin
of the world;
Have mercy upon *him*.
O Lamb of God, that takest away the sin
of the world;
Grant *him* Thy peace.

Amen.

EVERLASTING GOD, merciful Father,
Who tenderly carest for us in our need
and sorrow, and gavest Thy Son to be tempted
in all points like as we are, yet without sin,
that we might have a faithful High Priest
Who can be touched with the feeling of our
infirmities: We Thy children beseech Thee
for our afflicted *brother,* who lieth under Thy
mighty hand, that Thou wouldest not enter
into judgment with *him* for *his* sins, but
strengthen and comfort *him* by Thy Holy
Spirit in faith and patience, that *his* sickness
may be to Thy glory and the salvation of *his*
soul; through. . .

LITANY FOR THE DYING

LORD, have mercy.
  Lord, have mercy.
Christ, have mercy.
  Christ, have mercy.
Lord, have mercy.
  Lord, have mercy.

O GOD, the Father in Heaven
  Have mercy upon *him*.
O God, the Son, Redeemer of the world:
  Have mercy upon *him*.
O God, the Holy Ghost;
  Have mercy upon *him*.

Be gracious unto *him*.
  Spare *him,* good Lord.

Be gracious unto *him*.
  Help *him,* good Lord.

From Thy wrath;
From an evil death;   Good Lord,
From the pains of hell;   deliver
From the power of the devil;   *him*.
From all evil:

189

By Thy holy nativity;
By Thine agony and bloody
  sweat;
By Thy cross and passion;
By Thy death and burial;
By Thy glorious resurrection
  and ascension;
By the grace of the Holy
  Ghost, the Comforter:

} Help *him,*
good Lord.

In the hour of death;
And in the day of judgment;

} Help *him,*
good Lord.

We poor sinners do beseech Thee
  To hear us, O Lord God.

That Thou wouldest spare *him;*
  We beseech Thee to hear us, good Lord.

Lord, have mercy.
  Lord, have mercy.
Christ, have mercy.
  Christ, have mercy.
Lord, have mercy.
  Lord, have mercy.

Amen.

SOURCES

PREPARATORY COLLECTS

Lord if Thou art......................................*Anselm*
O Heavenly Father............................*Luther*
O Sacred Heart of Jesus......................*Roman*

COLLECTS AND PRAYERS

Brief Prayers and Aspirations

On Awaking
On Rising...........................No. 3, *John Cosin*
Before Divine Worship....No. 4,
                       Edward White Benson
After Divine Worship..............No. 2, *Jerome*
On Passing or Entering a Church
Before the Cross......................No. 2, *Jerome*
Before Reading Holy Scripture
On Beginning any Work
Grace before Meat
Thanksgiving after Meat
At Eventide
Before Sleep
    Most of the Aspirations are from Cardinal Bona's *Via Compendii ad Deum.*

COLLECTS

Adoration

O God Whom to know........................*Anselm*
Blessed be God........................*Sursum Corda*
To Jesus ....*Sursum Corda*
Spirit of Life...........................*Sursum Corda*
Glory to our Ascended Lord..*Sursum Corda*

Faith

Hope

Love

For Divine Aid in one's Calling

Lord God Thou hast placed................*Luther*
O God Almighty........*Greek Lit. of St. James*

For Grace to do one's Work

O God, Who hast commanded,
                   James Martineau
O Lord, give us the grace........*Henry Alford*
O God, the Sovereign Good,
                   William Bright

For the Holy Ghost

Heavenly King, Paraclete,
        Midnight Office, Greek Church
May the outpouring,*Gelasian Sacramentary*
Let Thy mercy...............................*Mozarabic*
O Merciful Lord...........................*Thomasius*
Almighty, Everlasting,
         Dionysius, the Carthusian

To Abound in Good Works
    Plant us in Thine house..................*Dionysius*

Before Reading Holy Scripture
    O Everlasting God................................*Luther*
    Almighty . . Whose Word,
                                    John Bugenhagen
    Lord Jesus, our King............................*Luther*
    O God, with Whom........................*Mozarabic*

After Reading Holy Scripture
    O God, Father of all mercies..............*Luther*
    Eternal Father..*Oestreich Kirchen Ordnung*

A Thanksgiving for the Holy Gospel
    We give thanks,
                        Oestreich Kirchen Ordnung

Before Study
    Almighty God, without........*Samuel Johnson*
    O God, Who hast..............*Samuel Johnson*
    O Thou, Who enlightenest..*Priest's Pr. Bk.*
    O Lord God, the Fountain............*P. Pr. Bk.*

Before Preparing a Sermon
    O God, the Holy Ghost
    Give me, O Teacher................*Henry S. Nash*
    O Lord and Saviour..............*William Bright*
    Meditation ....*Fulgentius*

For Illumination
    Let Thy mercy, O Lord..................*Mozarabic*

Lighten our eyes..............................*Mozarabic*
Almighty . . lighten ....*Dionysius*
Grant, O Lord..................................*Mozarabic*

For Faith

Almighty, Lord God
Braunschweig-Lueneberg Kirchen Ordnung
Almighty, Merciful..........*Saxe-Coburg K. O.*
We beseech Thee....*Leonine Sacramentary*

For Hope

May the hope....................................*Mozarabic*
Albeit, O Lord................................*Mozarabic*
O Lord, make us,
              Ludolphus, the Carthusian
It is good for us..............................*Mozarabic*

For Love

Confirm, O Lord..................................*Leonine*
O God, Who hast............................*Mozarabic*

For Heavenly Mindedness

Grant me ....*Leonine*

For Devout Mindedness

O Lord, with Whom........................*Mozarabic*

For Grace to Praise God

O God the Hope..............................*Thomasius*
O Lord Jesus Christ........................*Dionysius*
God, Who art..................................*Ludolphus*
Christ, the Lord..*Alcuin*

Almighty and Holy Spirit,
Philip Melanchthon

For Spiritual Communion

O God, the Health............................*Ludolphus*

For Wisdom

O God, Thou Who art....................*Ludolphus*
O Good Shepherd............................*Ludolphus*
O God, the Searcher........................*Dionysius*

To Pray Aright

O Lord, I beseech Thee.................*Leonine*
O Lord, Who seest....................*C. G. Rossetti*

For the Spirit of Prayer

O God of Hope.................................*Gelasian*

For Growth in Grace

O God, Who in.....................................*Leonine*

To Love Righteousness

Grant, Lord ....*Mozarabic*

For Consecration

O Holy Spirit....................................*Augustine*
Cause us, O Lord............................*Mozarabic*
Lord, do Thou turn me..........*Jeremy Taylor*
Living or dying, Lord..................*E. B. Pusey*

Self-surrender

Lord, take my lips................*W. H. H. Aitken*

To do God's Will
    O Good Jesus....................*Gregory, the Great*

For Purity of Heart
    O God, Who lovest all....................*Dionysius*

To Abound in Works of Mercy
    O Christ, our God............................*Mozarabic*

For Godly Life
    Make us, O Lord............................*Mozarabic*

For Grace to use one's Gifts
    O Lord God......................................*Ludolphus*

For Divine Guidance and Protection
    Grant us, O Lord................................*Gelasian*
    Grant . . unto us who........*Roman Breviary*
    O Lord, Keeper................................*Dionysius*
    Show Thy ....*Dionysius*
    O our King and God........................*Dionysius*
    Consider and hear............................*Mozarabic*
    O Lord Jesus Christ........................*Dionysius*
    Open . . Thy ears ....*Ludolphus*
    Of Thy merciful............................*Mozarabic*
    We beseech Thee..............................*Jerome*

Before a Journey
    O God, Who didst cause..............*Itinerarium*
    O God, Who didst bring..............*Itinerarium*
    Assist us ....*Itinerarium*
    Grant . . . that Thy family........*Itinerarium*

After a Safe Return
  Almighty . . Who Orderest

For Angelic Guard
  O God, Who..........................*Roman Breviary*

For Meekness
  Almighty . . grant that,
                    Gregorian Sacramentary
  O God, mercifully grant

Against Pride
  O Lord Most High..........................*Mozarabic*

To Rejoice in other Men's Success
  Almighty God give me............*Henry S. Nash*

Against a Froward Heart
  We sing of mercy...........................*Mozarabic*

For Obedience
  Make us of quick......................*C. G. Rossetti*

For Prudence
  Let wisdom ....*Mozarabic*

For Control of One's Tongue
  O Christ ....*Mozarabic*
  Almighty God ....*Ludolphus*
  Let our lips........................*Mozarabic, altered*
  We beseech Thee.............................*Jerome*
  O Lord, Most High.......................*Mozarabic*

Tongue and Lips
　We beseech Thee..........................*Gregorian*

Temper and Tongue
　O Lord, our Refuge................*C. G. Rossetti*

Secret Sins
　Almighty, Eternal God.....................*Gelasian*

For Deliverance from Temptation
　O Lord . . renew
　O Lord, my Support

For Victory in Temptation
　O God, the Might................*Roman Breviary*
　O Thou, Who in the wilderness
　Almighty God, the Preserver........*Ludolphus*
　O God, Who hast willed................*Mozarabic*

For Renewal
　We have walked..............................*Mozarabic*

In Trouble
　We call on Thee............................*Mozarabic*

In Adversity
　Redeem, O Lord..............................*Mozarabic*
　O God, be Thou ....*Mozarabic*
　O God, the Father ....*Mozarabic*
　O Lord, those are increased........*Mozarabic*
　Almighty, Everlasting God, *Lueneberg K. O.*

In Suffering
   O Thou, Who chastenest........*C. G. Rossetti*
   O God, Whose eyes........................*Mozarabic*

For Strength to Suffer and Persevere
   O Lord, let that become....*Thomas a Kempis*

In Cross Bearing
   O Lord, what cross......................*E. B. Pusey*

In Danger
   Grant . . that we ....*Roman Breviary*

In Persecution
   God, Who searchest......................*Thomasius*

In Deep Distress
   O Lord, let Thy mercy.................*Mozarabic*
   O Lord, Who didst..........................*Mozarabic*

Against Despair
   Almighty God, although...............*Mozarabic*

For Hope Amid Tribulation
   Hear us we beseech Thee........*Thomasius*

To Rejoice in God's Will toward us
   O God, Who chastenest......................*Leonine*

For Repentance
   O God, Incomprehensible..............*Ludolphus*

For Constancy
   Almighty and most Merciful........*Gregorian*

We know, O Lord..........................*Mozarabic*
O Christ ....*Mozarabic*

For Forgiveness

Cleanse us ....*Mozarabic*
We beseech Thee.........................*Mozarabic*
Hear us ....*Mozarabic*
O Lord, the Expectation................*Mozarabic*
We have sinned........*Monday Office, II Week
                    of the Fast, Greek Church*

After Receiving Absolution

Almighty, Everlasting,
                    Schwaebisch-Hall K. O.
Lord Jesus.......................................*Mozarabic*

For Peace

O God, our Refuge........................*Mozarabic*
Vouchsafe ....*Ludolphus*
O God, Who art Peace ....*Mozarabic*
O God, Who hast taught ....*Leonine*

That One's Prayer Be Heard

O Christ ....*Mozarabic*

Thanksgiving for Heard Prayer

O God, Whose mercy............*Loehe's Agenda*
O Lord, we beseech.............*Loehe's Agenda*

For Contentment

Grant, O Lord......................................*Leonine*
Almighty God ....*Oestreich K. O.*

FOR THE CHURCH

General

    Visit, O Lord....................................*Ludolphus*
    Almighty God..............*Acts of St. Damasius*
    O God, Whose Throne....................*Mozarabic*
    O Christ, the Word........................*Ludolphus*
    O Thou, Who art............................*Mozarabic*

In Time of Trial

    Let the sorrows

For the Propagation of the Gospel

    O Most Glorious..............................*Mozarabic*

For Christian Unity

    O God, our Father,
               Jacobite Liturgy of St. Dionysius

For the Parish Church......Common Ser. Book

For the Ministry

    Jesus, our Lord................................*Mozarabic*
    O Holy Lord..*Leonine*

For Men for the Ministry

    O Lord . . raise up..................*E. W. Benson*

For Those about to be Ordained

    O Lord, our God........*Ordinal, Greek Church*

For the Anniversary of Ordination

    O God, by Whose command..............*Gelasian*

For Synod
  Enlighten us
  O Almighty ....*P. Pr. Bk.*

For Missionaries
  O Lord Jesus Christ
  O Lord make ready

For Confirmands
  O God, Whose Spirit.........................*Gelasian*

For the Ministry of Mercy
  Most Merciful Father

FOR FAMILY AND FRIENDS

For a Family
  Almighty . . be Thou present..........*Gelasian*
  We beseech Thee.............................*Gelasian*
  O Almighty God........................*E. W. Benson*
  Bless, O God,
          Family Prayers, Ch. of Ireland

For One's Parents
  Almighty God.................................*John Cosin*

For One's Children
  Almighty God, the Father............*John Cosin*
  Almighty, Everlasting God....*Waldeck K. O.*
  O Lord Jesus Christ..................*E. W. Benson*

For a Friend
  O God, Who by the grace..............*Gregorian*
  Almighty . . have mercy ....*Gregorian*

For Brethren and Friends in Distant Lands
  Almighty Father........*Com. Prayer, Scotland*

For a Friend on His Birthday
  O God, the Life.....................*Gelasian*

FOR THE SICK

General
  Sovereign Lord..*Office for the Sick, Gk. Ch.*
  O God, Who ever...............*Gelasian*
  O God, Who hast...............*Gelasian*

Before Holy Communion for the Sick
  Almighty God . . since........*Loehe's Agenda*
  Almighty, Everlasting God,
        Visitation of the Sick, Waldeck K. O.
  Almighty God, Merciful........*Waldeck K. O.*
  Hear Me..........................*John Cosin*
  O Sweet Jesus..................*John Cosin*

Thanksgiving for Recovery from Sickness
  O God, in Whose hand

FOR THOSE FOR WHOM I SHOULD PRAY

For the Laborer
  Almighty God, Who.............*Oestreich K. O.*

For the Contrite
  O God, Who hast pity...................*Dionysius*

For the Outcasts
O God, Who tellest..............................*Sarum*

For the Distressed
Almighty and Everlasting................*Gelasian*

For the Afflicted
Unto every Christian,
                    Gk. Liturgy of St. Mark
We beseech........*Ambrosian Sacramentary*

For the Lapsed
O Lord God....................................*Mozarabic*

For the Iniquitous
O God, Who hatest..........................*Mozarabic*

For Unbelievers
Hear Thou ....*Mozarabic*

For Profaners of the Lord's Day
O God, grant................*Intercessory Manual*

For those who have none to pray for them
O Lord Jesus Christ....*Intercessory Manual*

In Old Age
O God, Unspeakable Mercy............*Dionysius*

For the Dying
Unto Thee ....*Gregorian*
Lord Jesus Christ............*Mozarabic Ordinal*

For a Happy Death
O God, Who art............................*Gallicanum*

For Those in Sorrow

O Heavenly Father..........*Com. Pr. Scotland*

In Commemoration of the Faithful Departed

Almighty God, with Whom,

Com. Pr. Scotland

O Almighty God...............*Com. Pr. Scotland*

GENERAL PRAYERS

Almighty and Merciful God...............*Alcuin*
O God, Thou art Life.........................*Anselm*
Lord, without Thee.....................*E. B. Pusey*
O God, the Father........*Gk. Lit. of St. James*
O Almighty God, give............*Jeremy Taylor*
O Thou Gracious.....................*Johann Arndt*
I offer up unto Thee........*Thomas a Kempis*
Ah, Lord, unto Whom............*Johann Arndt*
O God, my Everlasting......*James Martineau*
Give me, O Lord...........................*Gallicanum*
O God, to Whom...........................*Mozarabic*

MORNING PRAYERS

Lord's Day

Most Glorious Trinity..........*Loehe's Agenda*
O God, Who givest............*James Martineau*
From the night......*Daybreak Office, Gk. Ch.*
Grant us, O Lord...........................*Mozarabic*

General

O God, Who in...............................*Mozarabic*

O Merciful Lord God,
Primer of Henry VIII
Almighty God, Who............*Sarum Breviary*
Praised be Thou......*Morning Office, Gk. Ch.*
We give Thee thanks....*Gk. Lit. of St. Mark*
O Lord God...........................*Roman Breviary*
O Lord, our God....*Morning Office, Gk. Ch.*
Into the hands....................*Private Devotions*

From the Gelasianum

We give Thee thanks
Rising from our beds
O Lord, mercifully
O Lord, we humbly
Increase in us
O God, Who dividest
Send forth
Let Thy truth
We give unspeakable
God, Who dispellest
Graciously pour

EVENING PRAYERS

Lord's Day

Hail! gladd'ning Light, *Vesper Hymn, Gk.
Ch., IV Cent., John Keble, tr.*
In the evening.........*Vesper Office, Gk. Ch.*
O Lord God....................................*Mozarabic*
Watch over us.............*The Swedish Liturgy*

General

    O Lord, Who..........*Compline, Gk. Horology*
    O Lord, our......................................*John Cosin*
    Abide with us............................*E. W. Benson*
    Visit, we beseech...........*Augsberg Breviary*
    O Blessed God......................*James Martineau*
    O Lord, our God................................*Leonine*
    Be present ....*Gelasian*

Saturday Evening

    O Almighty God........................*E. W. Benson*

Before Going to Rest

    Ah Sweet Jesus...........................*Bonaventura*

Pillow-Prayers

    I commend myself......................*Bp. Andrews*
    God the Father................................*John Cosin*

IN PREPARATION FOR PARISH WORK

General

    Enlarge our souls................*James Martineau*
    Teach me...................................*Ignatius Loyola*
    O God..........................*Pocket Manual of Prs.*
    O Blessed Jesus..............................*H. S. Nash*

For Charity
    O God, Who

For Humility
    O God, Who raisest........................*P. Pr. Bk.*

For Consecration
  Lord God, the Holy Ghost
  Take our wills

For Moral Courage
  Grant us ....*P. Pr. Bk.*

For Earnestness
  Grant us . . spotless ....*P. Pr. Bk.*

For Perseverance
  O God, Who...................................*Gallicanum*
  Bless me, O God...............*Prs. for Students*

For Joy
  Who can be worthy.............................*Leonine*

For Ministerial Success
  O God, Who employest...................*P. Pr. Bk.*

For one's Parishioners
  O Eternal........*Michael Colium, Hanau K. u.*
                                    Schul Ord.

For the Children of the Parish
  Master and Saviour
  O Lord Jesus

For the Catechumens
  Almighty God.........................*Loehe's Agenda*

Before Bible School
  O Heavenly Father..........*Com. Pr. Scotland*
  O Almighty ....*Loehe's Agenda*

IN CONNECTION WITH DIVINE SERVICE

On Going to Church
 Lord, open

On Entering the Church
 O Lord, open Thou
 I believe in Thee
 Forgive, O God
 O God Whose Word

Before or after any Office
 O Merciful God
 Be present.....*Matthias, Bp. of Brandenburg*
  cir. 1540

In the Sacristy
 The God of our Lord,
 God and Master............*Gk. Lit. of St. James*
 Lord and Giver,
     Gk. Lit. of St. James (IV Cent.)
 We b. Thee....*Bp. Sarapion's Sacramentary*
 Lord, our God............*Coptic Lit. of St. Basil*
 Lord Jesu............................*Rituale u. Brevier*
 O Lord, my Gracious....*Gk. Lit. of St. James*
 O my God................................*St. Chrysostom*

While Vesting
 Cleanse me ....*Roman*
 Give me again.......................................*Roman*

As Occasion permits

Incline Thine ears....................................*Roman*
O God, to Whom.............................*Gregorian*
Let the Paraclete................................*Roman*
God, Who didst..............................*Gregorian*
Visit and cleanse................................*Roman*

For Choirs

O God, in Whose Temple..*Com. Pr. Scotland*
O God, to Whom

SHORT OFFICE BEFORE ENTERING THE SANCTUARY

In the Sanctuary

On Going to the Altar

Before the Altar

Forgive, O Lord

Before the Holy Gospel

O Lord and Lover

Gk. Lit. of St. Chrysostom

After the Holy Gospel

O God, Who..................*Gk. Lit. of St. James*

Before Preaching

O Lord Jesus....................................*P. Pr. Bk.*
Almighty ....*Leonine*
In the humility..............................*Mozarabic*

On Entering the Pulpit
After Preaching
  In Thy Name

Before Holy Communion
  O Holy Ghost
  We render............. .....*Gk. Lit. of St. James*
  O God, Who makest.......................*Ven. Bede*
  Count us worthy....*Sarapion's Sacramentary*
  We do not presume,
              First Pr. Bk. of Edward VI
  Creator of all things..........................*St. Cyril*
  Lord, I am not worthy..............*Bp. Andrews*
  Trusting only......................*Thomas a Kempis*
  O Lord, all.........................*Thomas a Kempis*
  O Lord Jesus Christ,
            Pfalz-Rhein, Bairn K. O.

An Epiklesis
  O God of Truth....*Sarapion's Sacramentary*
  Send down......................*Gk. Lit. of St. Mark*

At the Consecration
  One Holy..............*Clementine (Gk.) Liturgy*

Before Communing
  O God the Father........*Hannoverian Agenda*
  O Lord Jesus................*Hannoverian Agenda*

On Receiving the Bread
  Glory be to Thee........*Hannoverian Agenda*

On Receiving the Wine
  Glory be to Thee........*Hannoverian Agenda*

Thanksgiving after Communing
  Glory be to Thee................*Private Devotions*
  We give thanks..............................*Riga K. O.*
  Concerning the Eucharist..........*The Didache*
  Thou hast given............*Gk. Lit. of St. James*
  Ah, Jesus..........................*Manual of Devotion*
  Finished and accomplished,
                      Gk. Lit. of St. Basil

Before the Benediction
  I stretch out............*Sarapion's Sacramentary*

After the Benediction
  Going on from strength,
                      Gk. Lit. of St. James
  Grant, O Lord..........................*Scotch Liturgy*
  O God, the Life....................................*Gelasian*
  O Lord................................*Augsberg Breviary*

After the Service, in the Sacristy
  Most Blessed..........................*C. G. Diffenbach*
  O Lord God......................................*Gregorian*
  Forgive

On Leaving the Church
Before and after Vespers
  Jesus Master ....*Mozarabic*
  In Thy Most Holy............*Rituale u. Brevier*

LITANIES

Litany for Matins......................*Bp. Andrews*
Litany of the Most Holy Name of Jesus,
Roman—P. Pr. Bk.
Litany of the Passion..............*P. Pr. Bk. alt.*
Litany of the Holy Sacrament,
P. Pr. Bk. alt.
  Collect ....*Thomas Aquinas*
Litany of the Holy Ghost....*Loehe's Agenda*
  Collect................................*XVI Cent. K. O.*
Litany of Intercession
Litany for the Sick
Litany for the Dying
XVI Cent. K. O.—The Ch. Bk.
Litany for the Dying
XVI Cent. K. O.—The Ch. Bk.